Praise for *S*

"Many trauma survivors turn to ~~the communities~~ of faith first for support and healing. But some faith leaders fail to recognize the incredible privilege and responsibility of walking alongside hurting people and feel ill-equipped to do so. Even with the best of intentions, they may injure the trauma victim more deeply, effectively pushing them away from the God they seek. Dr. Christy Sim has provided a resource to help pastors understand the impact and reality of trauma and how best to help victims find safety, security, and healing. Every pastor should read this book and then keep it handy on the shelf for future reference for sources of help and information. This will become a 'must-read' for my classes."
—**Judith A. Schwanz**, Nazarene Theological Seminary, Kansas City, MO

"Sim gives voice to survivors in a call to churches to improve their understanding of and response to sexual and domestic violence. Her interest in linking trauma and neuroscience brings new understanding to the use of ritual, art, movement, and other body-centered practices for healing trauma in the context of faith communities."
—**Jeanne Hoeft**, Associate Professor of Pastoral Theology and Care, Saint Paul School of Theology, Leawood, KS

Survivor Care

WHAT RELIGIOUS PROFESSIONALS NEED TO KNOW ABOUT

Healing Trauma

Christy Gunter Sim

Survivor Care: What Religious Professionals Need to Know about Healing Trauma

The General Board of Higher Education and Ministry leads and serves The United Methodist Church in the recruitment, preparation, nurture, education, and support of Christian leaders—lay and clergy—for the work of making disciples of Jesus Christ for the transformation of the world. The General Board of Higher Education and Ministry of The United Methodist Church serves as an advocate for the intellectual life of the church. The Board's mission embodies the Wesleyan tradition of commitment to the education of laypersons and ordained persons by providing access to higher education for all persons.

The Wesley's Foundery Books is an imprint of the General Board of Higher Education and Ministry, The United Methodist Church, and named for the abandoned foundery that early followers of John Wesley transformed, which later became the cradle of London's Methodist movement.

HIGHER EDUCATION & MINISTRY
General Board of Higher Education and Ministry
THE UNITED METHODIST CHURCH

This book is dedicated to all those who felt they were thrown out in the church's trash and to the holy men and women who want to do better.

———

Holy Communion

*I loved Jesus so much
I once rescued
communion wafers
from the trash
and sprinkled them onto the earth.*

*The cardinals feasted on them through winter.
Years later, holy men put me in the trash.
No one came to my rescue
So
I went back to the dirt.*
—Marie Thearose

Contents

Introduction

Recently I asked an important question on one of my social media pages. My purpose was to hear from survivors with experiences different from my own. I expected around twenty responses. Instead, I received more than six hundred replies. I asked, "If you could tell your pastor one thing, what would it be?" Most of the survivors' stories were painful to read. I heard things like:

> "My church helped me in some ways, but some of the leaders and staff advised me to stick it out with my abuser and go to counseling. It just made things worse."

> "I wish my pastor took a moment to feel my broken heart with me instead of assuming I was crazy or exaggerating."

> "Don't think your church is exempt. It's happening in your pews."

> "Stop with the useless words. Like 'everything happens for a reason.' Why in the world would I be assaulted for a reason? I don't appreciate that, God."

> "When you're preaching about forgiveness, you should really remember us. Put an exception in what you're saying. Always remember the woman who is being abused at home."

"Remember the words 'It's OK' are ridiculous. I'm not OK. Someone I love violated me. It's never going to be fully OK again."

"Don't dismiss me because you think my abuser is a great person. Of course, they are a great person around *you*."

"What caused me the most pain was dealing with church leaders who didn't believe I suffered so much. When the church leaders didn't believe me, I had a hard time believing it happened. I mean, maybe I am just too dramatic (or whatever else). And when I couldn't believe it, I couldn't heal. I need you to believe me more than you can imagine."

"Why do you hold me more accountable than my abuser? Try holding him accountable instead."

"Seminary does not qualify you to deal with the extensiveness of abuse or chronic trauma. Get community support. You're not a trauma expert."

"I really wish you didn't demand I forgive. I was traumatized; forgiveness wasn't on my radar . . . and it won't be for a long time."

"I never want to walk into a church again. I can't even answer this question because I was harmed so significantly."

"You made the abusive situation so much worse. Do you even realize how much damage you did?"

This kind of response, six hundred times over, shows a gap between what we intend to do (love and care for the people in our congregations) and what survivors are experiencing. We would be wise to hear the voices of those sharing their painful stories and learn from them. So many survivors have been harmed by their community, the place that was supposed to be safe and loving.

This book was written with an intent to show the many ways survivors of domestic violence and sexual assault feel ignored, devalued, humiliated, and shamed in their faith communities.

Within this book their vulnerability and personal stories of harm are carefully considered and valued. It is my hope that I was faithful in deeply listening to those who have experienced what I have not.

If you pay attention, you can hear what I hear survivors saying every day: "Change is needed. I've been hurt by my community. They didn't believe me. They thought I was too dramatic. They thought he was too nice to hurt me." Those who feel this type of negative reaction and poor response from churches urge us to hear their collective voice. You are invited to empathize with the pain and learn how to offer healing responses to violence. We can do better, and this book will show how.

How to Be Trauma Informed

At the 2017 National Sexual Assault Conference in Dallas, Texas, Julie Germann, a former prosecutor, spoke in a plenary session. She talked about how difficult it was to prosecute cases of domestic violence and sexual assault. She asked herself why it was so hard. Why were these more difficult than any other case? What was the "it" that made it feel as if she was "swimming in mud"?

Before long the answer came to her. What made domestic violence and sexual assault cases so difficult, she decided, was that she was constantly fighting the very people who were supposed to be on her side. Germann claimed she felt as if she was constantly battling her allies.

Law enforcement would ask, "Can we just drop this case?" and she would have to fight to prosecute it. A judge would say, "I think what she was wearing is relevant to this case," and Germann would contest that assertion to prove women are not to blame for assault, no matter what they are wearing. Germann said fighting all these people who were supposed to be on her side made her job incredibly difficult.

As I listened to this presentation I started chuckling to myself, not because it was funny, but because my life suddenly started to make more sense. This is exactly my own story, but instead of the

3

criminal justice system, my "swimming in mud" happens in the church. Pastors say, "I dropped her off at the shelter and she just went back to him. I'm done helping her"; or, "Why can't she just leave him?" I have to fight to help pastors understand this behavior is completely normal and, truthfully, expected. A Christian counselor will suggest couples therapy (when there are obvious power and control issues). I wade through explaining why this is often a dangerous and terrible idea. Just like the prosecutor, fighting allies—those who are supposed to be on my side to care for survivors of horrific trauma—makes my job so hard. In both of these situations with a pastor and Christian counselor, trauma-informed care is needed.

But it is not just me fighting this battle and feeling frustration. Those who work for the civic and social agencies that exist to help survivors get irritated as well. Professionals who understand the neurobiology of trauma and typical victim behavior also experience the feeling of "swimming through mud." We watch as survivors are forced to work through secondary trauma caused by their faith communities, which can often be more painful than the original abuse. Once a victim finally grasps the notion that a person they love can cause incredible harm, there tends to be an expectation that the people of God will be different (and we should be).

We all agree that domestic violence and sexual assault are horrendous experiences. However, religious professionals and counselors sometimes want to separate the trauma from faith issues. How all of us respond to these issues varies significantly, but there needs to be a balance, a way to meet the spiritual needs of survivors and provide trauma-informed response.

We need to work together to offer spiritual care in a trauma-informed way. In the church, as well as in social and civic spaces, our response to survivors of domestic violence and sexual assault must include being knowledgeable about the physiology of trauma. This book will both teach what to expect in the trauma response and guide you in how to respond appropriately.

How to Work with Community Partners

There is incredible work going on in every state, helping survivors find hope and healing in shelters and service provision agencies. Religious professionals can partner with these civic and social organizations to be even stronger in how we provide spiritual care to survivors.

I have been a pastor and was ordained as an elder who served as both a children's pastor and a senior pastor. I have walked with people through hospital visits, funerals, and baptisms; and I have dealt with angry parishioners. I have also worked at the state level with domestic violence and sexual assault providers to analyze service provision. I have seen the inside view of many different types of civic/social service providers in multiple states. I have interviewed advocates and read and designed more policies and procedures than I can count. I have worked with governing boards and more. I understand the church wants to provide the best care to people, and I am familiar with the responsibilities of the agencies funded by the government. This book will help you navigate the difficult space of helping survivors by knowing how to interact with your community partners.

Over the years I have watched far too many churches destroy a relationship with their local family violence agencies because they were simply unaware of basic requirements of confidentiality and survivor-centered services. This book can help you understand why a pastor might feel frozen out by a local family violence service provider. There are certain behaviors required of service providers to remain eligible to receive government funding and stay open. These are requirements you may not know and might be surprised to learn. This book will help translate the civic and social responsibilities to the language of faith space.

Why Our Response to Survivors Matters

Domestic violence and sexual assault are huge problems, even in faith communities. No matter how much we are convinced otherwise, our divorce rates are still the same as the public at large, and our family violence statistics are identical to those in the rest of the nation. The Center for Disease Control tells us that one in every three women will be assaulted in her lifetime.[1] That means one out of every three women in your pews has firsthand experience with this trauma. It is a massive problem that is entirely too common.

Not so long ago, divorce was a taboo topic in nearly every church. It still is an unmentionable topic in many communities, but churches finally have started discussing the complexities of that issue. In the same way conversations about divorce opened up, we need to think critically about issues related to family violence. If we can start to talk about violence and how it creeps into our churches right under our noses, we can begin to get a sense of the patterns and learn the basics of offering beneficial care for survivors.

The voices of survivors, however, tell us they are not always encountering healthy responses, especially in church. Instead, they find their church taking sides with the abuser, forcing the survivor to take responsibility for a divorce, or not being believed about the severity of the abuse they report. This leaves survivors alone and isolated in their journey for healing, causing secondary trauma.

In my world, where I deal with survivors of violence daily, I see women in particular leaving the church in order to find healing elsewhere. The space that should be welcoming, loving, and supportive becomes a source of greater agony and pain. Therefore, this book was written to help leaders access the tools

---

1   CDC, "Intimate Partner Violence," accessed Dec. 30, 2017, www.cdc.gov /violenceprevention/intimatepartnerviolence/index.html.

needed to reduce the amount of secondary harm churches inflict upon survivors of violence. It is time to pay attention to this crucial issue in our faith communities, and this book is a guide for how to do that.

How to Be Survivor Informed

As the domestic violence and intimate partner violence movement grows, we are seeing a shift from victims leading the movement to experts and professionals taking center stage. When the domestic violence movement first started in the late 1970s and early 1980s in the United States, survivors led a grassroots movement. They provided the safe houses and fought for legislative reform. As the decades have passed, however, the victims, while still leading as advocates, are often replaced in higher-level positions by experts such as social workers, attorneys, and executives. The movement has turned into a professional field.

Although I deeply appreciate the work and voices of those who *support* survivors of violence, those who *have lived through* the experience of domestic violence and sexual assault must be included in this movement, despite the institutionalizing of the field. Everything we do must be informed by the needs of current and past survivors. This is such an important piece of my own philosophy of pastoral care for victims of domestic violence and sexual assault. Even though I am a survivor myself, I must practice deep listening too.

Many years ago, I wrote a poem while seeking protection in a domestic violence shelter. As a resident, it was my responsibility to clean the chapel. After I wiped down each Celtic cross, reorganized the pamphlets, and dusted the altar, I would sit down and cry, wondering how I went from being the pastor in the pulpit to this.

One of those nights, a church leader told me, not for the first time, that I would be fine. "Everything is going to be OK," he said. But I knew better. I was coming "home" to a house full of other traumatized women where I had to wash clothes based on when I was scheduled, with a detergent I did not pick, and I ate only if I made it back to the dining room in time. There were no snacks allowed in my room, and I once got written up for cleaning my bathroom counter with a Lysol wipe (which can be used as drugs, apparently). Even my toothpaste was different. In the midst of upheaval I sought some familiarity. I wanted my slippers, a solid pillow to sleep on, a feeling of *normal*.

Just weeks before entering the shelter I was held against my will, violated, and terrorized in ways many people cannot imagine. Then I found myself sitting in the chapel of a domestic violence shelter. Nothing would ever be fully OK again, no matter what a church leader said.

Somehow, miraculously, the poem I composed that day survived beyond that night and even evolved through the years. Although I am now an expert in the field of trauma and abuse, I will never forget the days that were the source of such a raw and vulnerable poem.

In order to keep my own narrative in the forefront of my memory, I hold this poem close, along with the letter from the shelter that declared me homeless. Both are framed in my office. I hold and honor the memories of these traumatic experiences as guidance for the survivors living in the midst of violence now. This is important and helps me keep my own survivor voice at the center, even as an expert.

The poem I wrote that day in the chapel is included here, in this introduction. I share it as a model of viewing domestic violence and sexual assault through the lens of a survivor. I would not be able to recapture something like this now. Thus, I urge you to join me and keep these painful moments in the forefront as you read this book. Let it be your "framed letter." I hope it will help keep us survivor centered and trauma informed.

That night, crumpled up on a chair in the safe house chapel, I wrote these words as a very fresh victim of violence:

In the terror of absence
And emptiness of night,
She coughs out nothing but air,
Not enough strength to add words to a prayer.

Gagging from memories,
Collapsing from pain,
She takes another shallow breath,
Spewing her spiritual insides to its death

And yet you say, "Someday, some way, everything's
    going to be okay."
You say, "Redemption is calling, hope is still ablaze."
You say, "There's stillness and peace."
That "someday, some way, all this agony will cease."

But for her on this night,
In these moments of difficulty, these places of grief,
What she needs, what she reminds, is you're the hope.
To become the answer to her prayer.

Because tonight, right now,
There's bile of anguish rising on her tongue.
Those words of hope are empty and shallow,
Nothing but worthless and hollow.

What she needs, what she reminds
Is you're the one
Called to bring balance and hope,
Providing enough balm to survive this night and cope

Because tonight doesn't feel like it's going to be okay,
And tonight doesn't feel alright.

And yet you still say, "Someday, some way, everything's
    going to be okay."
You say, "Redemption is calling, hope is still ablaze."

You say, "There's stillness and peace."
That "someday, some way, all this agony will cease."

Imagine the kind of pain that makes you spew out your emotional insides and memories that make you gag. This is the level of agony a victim of violence experiences. It is terrible. These voices must be kept center stage as you read this book in order to stay survivor informed.

This Book Is for You

This book is for pastors, faith leaders, counselors, and anyone who offers care in religious or congregational settings; but it is also for those who offer care as part of their ministry, for example, in hospitals, on college campuses, or in the armed forces. If you encounter any people at all, statistics indicate that you are working with folks who have experienced or who are currently experiencing domestic violence and sexual assault.

According to the 2014 Lifeway Research Project sponsored by Sojourners and IMA World Health, "Pastors and Domestic and Sexual Violence," 60 percent of pastors believe that 20 percent of adults in the United States have been victims of domestic and sexual violence.[2] The actual statistics for women are much higher than the majority believes. The Center for Disease Control reports that 1 in 3 women (33 percent) in the United States have experienced some form of sexual violence during their lifetime;[3] 1 in 4 women have been the victim of severe physical violence by a

---

2   LifeWay Research, "Pastors and Domestic and Sexual Violence, Survey of 1,000 Protestant Pastors," sponsored by Sojourners and IMA World Health, conducted May 7–31, 2014.

3   Findings from the National Intimate Partner and Sexual Violence Survey, 2010–2012 State Report Fact Sheet, accessed February 22, 2018, www.cdc.gov/violenceprevention/pdf/NISVS-StateReportFact sheet.pdf.

partner; and 1 in 9 men were victims of contact sexual violence, physical assault, and/or stalking by an intimate partner.[4]

The church is filled with people who experience domestic violence and sexual assault. When a pastor learns about the violence, it can become the scariest moment in their life. Even picking up this book is intimidating for some. But this book will help you to gain power over that fear and be equipped with the tools you need in these situations.

How to Use This Book

In chapter 1 you will develop a foundation for understanding the basic framework of domestic violence and sexual assault with definitions and concepts. These are notions that involve trauma, autonomy, and violence. The overarching purpose of this chapter is to lay the groundwork for the following chapters by explaining the basic concepts of domestic violence and sexual assault.

Chapter 2 will help you begin to understand normal victim responses by reviewing the brain's and body's response to trauma. This chapter should give you the tools to understand what is happening in the body physically during a traumatic experience. This second chapter will be helpful for all our work with those who suffer, beyond issues of violence. Trauma can occur during any stage of life, and this chapter can help with many issues faith leaders encounter when providing pastoral care.

In chapter 3 you will encounter notions of healing and receive an overview of the concept of "thriving" by Thema Bryant-Davis. This chapter also incorporates Sharon Stanley's work on the process of how healing happens after trauma. The purpose of chapter 3 is to provide a framework for understanding healing based on

---

4 Findings from the National Data on Intimate Partner Violence, Sexual Violence, and Stalking, accessed February 22, 2018, www.cdc.gov /violenceprevention/pdf/NISVS-Fact-Sheet-2014.pdf. To view the infographic, see www.cdc.gov/violenceprevention/nisvs/summaryreports .html (accessed April 5, 2018).

brain and body trauma. Our healing methods must be informed by what we know about the physiological response to trauma. If you enjoy science, chapters 2 and 3 should be a real treat for you. As I worked on these components, I had a neuroscientist review them for accuracy. Chapter 3 is also where you will encounter foundations for healing and find recommendations for how healing tools and techniques look for survivors of violence.

In chapter 4 you will learn about the importance of caring for yourself while you stand with a person in crisis. This chapter will be helpful for all types of trauma dealt with in pastoral care, not just violence. Additionally, this chapter will empower you to develop tools that enable you to be aware of your own internal experience, identify triggers, know your bias, and understand your own physiological response.

Secondary trauma has certain signs and symptoms to watch for, and, furthermore, chapter 4 will help you know how to create an individual plan for self-care and develop a framework for an organization's plan for self-care. There are measures you can take *before* you are in the experience of walking with someone in trauma, things you can do *during* the experience, and follow-up tools you can use *after* the experience. Knowing how and when to utilize these tactics is an important step to self-care.

In this chapter I also delve into thinking through the faith leader's power and privilege as they walk alongside a vulnerable population such as survivors of violence. There are important things we need to think about as those who hold power in a relationship with a victim of violence or assault.

In chapter 5 you will become familiar with the work of community partners who provide direct services to survivors of violence. This chapter provides a framework for understanding how the church can be in a healthy relationship with civic agencies. Confidentiality is discussed in this chapter as well, as are the expected standards of care that are trauma informed and survivor centered. You will also learn about the various grants that fund your local

service provider and become aware of their requirements for continued funding. Be aware: some of the actions and words you
hear from your local agency might seem offensive to you but are
requirements to continue providing twenty-four-hour hotlines, safe
shelter, counseling, advocacy, and more to survivors of violence.

Overall this chapter will help faith leaders know what is and
is not expected of them, and especially when it is time to refer.
Often the needs of the victim far outweigh the abilities of the
faith community, and it is important for faith leaders to understand what they can and cannot do for survivors.

Finally, in chapter 6, you will learn basic tools for preparing for
a church crisis, including child custody issues or the threat of an
active shooter. As the 2017 Baptist church shooting in southern
Texas made very clear, mass shootings in faith communities are,
all too often, directly connected to family violence. Therefore, the
book will end with tools and resources for preparing for such a
crisis in the faith community.

As my favorite police chief with whom I work to train churches
for such safety issues, Chief Anthony Williams, often says at train-
ings: "If it is foreseeable, it is preventable." And as my colleague
Dr. Rev. Mike Sneed says, "It doesn't matter how large or small
your church is, it matters how safe you want your church to be."[5]
With the wisdom of the core group of trainers from AIMS Training and Consulting, which includes Chief Anthony Williams; Dr.
William "Edward" Smith, DT; Marieta Oglesby, MLS, CCP; and
Chaplain James Bradley, DCCCD PD, chapter 6 will empower us
to ensure our churches are safe places.

Throughout the entire book, readers will find:

Case Studies
   • To practice thinking through how you can
     improve your response to violence and practically
     apply the new concepts.

---

5   See www.aimsconsulting-training.com/church-safety-seminars.html.

Top 10s
- To give you steps and ideas for dealing with a particular issue. These include topics such as the top 10 things to ask yourself in order to know if you are ready to help a victim in trauma, my top 10 recommendations for when you are subpoenaed to testify in family court, and the top 10 things you can do for survivors.

Reference Guide
- To provide quick reference pages on the go. These address issues such as understanding the basics of active listening, how to de-escalate a situation, and a crisis-moment checklist.

Disclaimers and Appreciation

As you read through these chapters, please know I am not an expert on child abuse, violence against older adults, service provision to the disabled community, or many other topics. I do not go into detail about prison or offender rehabilitation. I do not describe things like the Adverse Childhood Experiences research or the micro and macro aggressions toward the LGBTQ community. There is much that surrounds issues of domestic violence and sexual assault, truly more than I could fit into this work. I carefully picked from a massive amount of information what I heard survivors say was most important for faith leaders to know when working with domestic violence and sexual assault victims.

If there are topics important to you that are not found in this book, seek resources that do have the information you need. There are many survivors and experts who are invested in this work who can help guide you through this journey. Note that names, places, and identifying factors were changed or altered to protect the confidentiality of those involved. Thank you for joining me through the experience of reading this book. Together we can make a difference for the survivors of violence.

1

Forming a Basis for Understanding Domestic Violence and Sexual Assault Victims

It was a chilly spring afternoon when I got a call from an unknown number. I was relaxed on the couch, laughing with my kids, when I heard a whisper on the other line: "Christy, help me." I sat up quickly and tried to figure out who was on the other line. She continued: "I had to run away again, and no one from church would give me your number." I kept listening. "So, I walked a few miles home so I could find your contact information and call." She spoke with agony and suffering in her tone: "I finally got ahold of you anyway. Now that I have, can you come meet me?"

In those moments, there were several thoughts going through my heart and mind. I could gather a lot of information from this short phone call.

1. The caller was living in a domestic violence shelter again.
2. She wanted to talk to someone who understood the dynamics of trauma and intimate partner violence, but her church would not give her my phone number to do so.
3. She walked miles (and entered a location where she had just been violently assaulted) to get my number.
4. The church community's response put her in a position of increased vulnerability and caused her secondary trauma.

In the moments of this type of experience, I learned, well-intentioned, loving people in the church community do not yet understand the dynamics of chronic trauma or how our responses can cause more harm than we ever believed.

This story is not unique. Unfortunately, it is quite common, with perhaps just a few changes in the details. The most common response from church leaders to this story is: "I would never do that. I wouldn't cause additional harm." However, I urge you to set aside that thought. The folks to whom I am referring in this story gave of their hearts, finances, and resources to help this young lady. They were good people. But when things got terrible, as domestic violence situations usually do, they decided to "not play into her delusions" and to give her "tough love." Their idea of helping was to refuse her access to me. They thought they were doing the right thing. They thought I, as an advocate, would just enable her right back into her situation.

These good church people watched this young woman leave her abusive partner multiple times, and they helped her out of dozens of situations. However, since they were not as trauma informed as they could have been, their choice of words and actions were the worst possible response for this victim.

As Russell Strand, retired senior special agent in the US Army Criminal Investigations Command and managing partner and cofounder of Strand Holistic Innovative Forensic Techniques[1] said in a training in 2017: "There's not much we can do to make it better. But there's a whole lot we can do to make it worse."[2] I find myself offering this same advice to pastors in consultations quite frequently. You cannot fix the situation; you cannot make it all better. But there is so much you can do to make it worse.

---

1   Russell Strand (lecture, Turning Point Rape Crisis Center at the Collin County Court House, McKinney, TX, May 26, 2017). See more at www .russellstrand.com.

2   Strand lecture.

This chapter will help to develop a framework for understanding the basics of domestic violence and sexual assault with definitions and concepts that will enable us to build a foundation for learning how not to cause further harm in our responses. But first let us turn to some basics about trauma.

Trauma Defined

Trauma is an overwhelming experience where a person perceives a closeness to death, cannot cope in the moment, no action is imaginable, agency is lost, a sense of meaning is violated, and the body's alert system is activated for further survival in similar situations. Violence and abuse are terrible experiences for anyone to live through. They are horrific, causing deep and emotional distress. Quite often, the experience of violence can be a traumatic experience for victims.

There are several key identifying factors to understanding trauma. These are things you, as a faith leader, should watch for in your pastoral care. In the trauma experience:

1. Victims Perceive They Are Close to Death

According to Marie Marshall Fortune, an act of violence is "an act of . . . hatred, and aggression."[3] What Fortune finds crucial to the experience of violence is what she describes as the victim believing they will die. She says, "Whether or not physical violence was inflicted, the most common reaction of a victim who experienced trauma is, 'I thought I was going to be killed.' "[4] Violence is about hate toward another human to the point one wishes they ceased to exist.

Note this experience is more about the perception of how close one is to death than the actuality of being close to death.

---

3   Marie Marshall Fortune, *Sexual Violence: The Unmentionable Sin* (New York: Pilgrim, 1983), 5.
4   Fortune, 5.

As tempting as it might be to believe death was not imminent for the victim, no one other than the victim can decide if they feel death is looming. It is only the victim's perception of impending death that determines if trauma occurred. However, this is not to say trauma is only in the mind or that those who survive violence were crazy to think they would die. In my experience with survivors, if they perceived a potential for death, they were correct. The perpetrator was behaving in a murderous manner and could have killed them. Whenever a person believes they could die, that needs to be taken seriously. They know their life situation. They know how quickly the tide can turn. My point is that even if the person was not actually close to death in their experience of violence and abuse, trauma can still occur. Feeling like death is possible, looking at a person and believing they want to kill you, creates this first key factor of identifying a horrendous abusive situation, terrible enough to be called "trauma." This trauma happens when the victim perceives they are close to death.

It is also important to note the experience of a closeness to death could mean something other than being physically killed. It could mean the death of something important for survival, as when someone experiences a disconnect from their community. It could mean a death in reputation and career, in one's ability to make an impact on the world, if that is crucial to survival. Therefore, I propose there are two ways to think about perceiving closeness to death in trauma:

- Perceiving closeness to a physical death where breath ends and the body stops
- Perceiving closeness to a social death regarding connections for survival

One or both of these could be present for the experience to be traumatic.

2. The Experience Is Overwhelming

Trauma is a wordless, unspeakable, and overwhelming experience. I often talk about traumatic events in terms of something that happens when we are unable to assign language to the experience. Stephanie Covington, author of the book and accompanying workbook *Beyond Trauma: A Healing Journey for Women*, says: "Trauma is any stressor that occurs in a sudden and forceful way and is experienced as overwhelming."[5] In other words, trauma is not a crisis moment that intensifies and resolves. Trauma is intrusive and overwhelms. The experience takes over the capacity to deal with the intensity of the moment. Therefore, it is unspeakable and difficult to find words to describe.

Judith Herman's classic work *Trauma and Recovery* describes in detail the overwhelming experience of trauma. "Traumatic events are extraordinary," she writes, because "they overwhelm the ordinary human adaptions to life" in that they "confront human beings with the extremities of helplessness and terror and evoke the responses of catastrophe."[6] In other words, trauma involves attempting to run, fight, or engage social connection (all the normal coping mechanisms for survival) and not being able to act or change how the experience happens. There is a sense of helplessness to act, as they are completely overwhelmed by what is happening to them.

3. Agency Is Lost Because No Action Is Imaginable

On the same trajectory, Herman explains that "traumatic reactions occur" when there is no action imaginable, when neither

---

5   Stephanie Covington, *Beyond Trauma: A Healing Journey for Women* (Participant's Workbook) (Center City, MN: Hazelden, 2003), 4.

6   Judith Herman, MD, *Trauma and Recovery: The Aftermath of Violence—from Domestic Abuse to Political Terror* (New York: Perseus, 1992), 33.

"resistance nor escape is possible."[7] Thus, a trauma moment happens when the victim cannot fight back or run away; there is no escape, and that overwhelming sense of dread becomes more than just a feeling. The victim has no options, no choices, and no action is imaginable. Thus, I add to this a third qualifier: in trauma moments, agency is lost.

In crisis, our fight/flight/freeze response is activated. If the crisis persists, we can employ one of these responses to act. We can run away, we can fight back, or we can get ready to fight or run. But in trauma, no action is possible. We cannot run or fight. Our sense of agency to affect our experience disappears. Herman continues later to describe "traumatic events" as violating the very "autonomy of the person."[8] Thus, when a person loses the ability to either run away or fight back, they have lost their agency. They lose their ability to exercise any control over the outcome of the experience. They cannot leave; they cannot make it stop. They are trapped in the moment without agency or choice.

Fortune adds to this discussion of agency by her claim that even "the power to decide, to choose, to determine, to consent or withhold consent in the most concrete bodily dimension, all vanish."[9] She backs up this point by noting trauma happens when the victim cannot control their body or what is happening to them. There is no power, no autonomy, and no ability to control their involvement in the experience; thus, it is a traumatic event.

4. A Sense of Meaning Is Lost and Violated

When meaning is violated in the traumatic experience, several things might happen:

---

7   Herman, 34.
8   Herman, 52.
9   Fortune, *Sexual Violence*, 6–7.

- A view of being safe in the world could shift.
- The person begins to feel isolated, and thus the experience of community changes.
- They begin to question themselves and their competence in the world.
- The person might question the divine's ability to act in the world.

Herman explains that "traumatic events . . . shatter the sense of connection," often "creating a crisis of faith" and belief in a meaningful world.[10]

Herman also asserts that a survivor of trauma is left with a crisis of trust. She claims that "the belief in a meaningful world" is crucial, and to lose this faith in the order of the universe is devastating.[11] This is especially true when the loss involves trust in someone you love. To lose your faith in a person you love and trust can paralyze you for a long time.

Often the person's own perceptions become a clouded mess of confusion. Victims doubt themselves; they doubt others; and they tend to be overwhelmed with perplexing feelings about meaning. It is all quite confusing and difficult to process.

Trauma is so overwhelming, violating, and intrusive for victims that it makes them question their confidence in the world around them and wonder if their life has value. Victims of abuse and violence frequently begin to question purpose. They have been violated in the deepest sense of humanity. The meaning and value they find in connection to others are often crushed.

The Result of Trauma on the Body

After experiencing various parts of these four aspects that make up a traumatic experience, the person is left with deep changes in the body. I summarize these changes in four ways. Trauma

---

10 Herman, *Trauma and Recovery*, 54–56.
11 Herman, 55.

leaves: a death imprint, an active alert system, a changed body, and an instinctual need to heal and resolve. These four aspects are discussed in more detail below.

1. Trauma Leaves a Death Imprint

After a traumatic experience, victims are forced into functioning in an alternative way that focuses on survival from anything similar to the violence they lived through. Their behavior is affected to the point they feel the need to maintain constant vigilance against potential threat. The person has experienced the fear they will die, they were overwhelmed in their capacity to respond, lost all sense of agency, and have begun to question meaning and value. To suffer this kind of impact results in significant changes to how a person's body protects itself in the future.

Herman claims, "After a traumatic experience, the human system of self-preservation seems to go onto permanent alert, as if the danger might return at any moment."[12] These phenomena can plague a person for a very long time, and life changes drastically in the future for the survivor, as their body attempts to protect itself from ever feeling this again. Herman goes on to argue that after violence the person no longer has "a normal 'baseline' level of alert but relaxed attention" in that "their bodies are always on the alert for danger."[13] Herman then quotes Robert Jay Lifton, calling this phenomenon a "death imprint,"[14] which means that the danger alert system is overstimulated. "When high levels of adrenaline and other stress hormones are circulating," Herman writes, "memory traces are deeply imprinted."[15] In other words, after trauma, the perception of impending and potential death is imprinted deep within a person's cells. After a traumatic experience, a person's body changes and is newly

---

12 Herman, 35.
13 Herman, 36.
14 Herman, 38.
15 Herman, 39.

focused on survival, protecting the body from anything similar to the horror they experienced that brought them close to physical and/or social death.

2. Trauma Leaves an Active Alert System

Therefore, we can say that after trauma, the normal alert response is gone and is replaced by an exaggerated and active response to the death imprint. The aftermath of trauma is marked with a hyperactive alert system that is searching for potential threat.

Dr. Lenore Walker, advocate and researcher of domestic violence, refers to this trauma response as "anxiety," which is basically "a call to danger."[16] A survivor of violence is on constant psychological and mental alert, watching for signs of danger. The survivor experienced the trauma of not being able to respond, perceived impending death, and now they are often trapped in this threat-alert response mode. Their bodies are imprisoned in this alternative response—watching for any potential for a similar danger.

Bessel van der Kolk, a medical doctor and expert in trauma healing, describes the part of the brain that is on constant alert for danger. In the brain there are various systems enabling the body to survive. One of these is the limbic system, which is a "term for a group of interconnected structures" that are "concerned with emotions and memory."[17] Van der Kolk adds that within the limbic system is the amygdala; this part of the brain's purpose is to search for danger.[18] It is the amygdala that is constantly searching for threat. I will discuss this in more detail in subsequent chapters.

---

16 Lenore E. Walker, *The Battered Woman* (New York: Harper Perennial, 1979), 51.

17 Ken Ashwell, *The Brain Book: Development, Function, Disorder, Health* (Buffalo, NY: Firefly, 2012), 34.

18 For more information on the limbic system, see: https://www.nicabm .com/trauma-how-limbic-system-therapy-can-help-resolve-trauma/.

3. Trauma Changes the Body

After the experience of violence and trauma, a person's body changes. The brain, specifically the amygdala, has an altered purpose. It is looking for a specific type of danger. Hormones are released when threat is detected, and those hormones affect behavior. The body and brain changed because of violence. Part of the intense struggle after the traumatic experience is trying to understand and make sense of what your body is now doing. This will be discussed in further detail in chapter 2.

4. Trauma Creates an Instinctual Need to Heal and Resolve

As a result of this altered body response, the person often relives the experience again and again. We call this retrieval of the experience "flashbacks" that happen over and over, as if by so doing, it will "change the outcome of the dangerous encounter."[19] The body and brain of the person flash back to the trauma moment and feel it repeatedly. Herman claims this involuntary or voluntary reliving experience is an "attempt at healing."[20] Unfortunately, such repetition does not promote healing. Flashbacks, the body's natural response, tend not to assist the healing process. They simply serve to keep the body out of a similar traumatic experience. Instead, Herman advises, "the trauma is resolved only when the survivor develops a new mental 'schema' for understanding what has happened," which is often resisted, dreaded, and feared.[21] To heal, victims must find a way to exit the normal body process and walk into that which they want to resist, that which they often fear.

When a person experiences a trauma flashback, it is a natural response to attempt self-healing. But the way healing actually

---

19 Herman, *Trauma and Recovery*, 36.
20 Herman, 41.
21 Herman, 41–42.

progresses is not often instinctual or the automatic response. Instead, victims continue to relive the trauma experience until another force is acted upon it. In other words, healing becomes possible when a person intentionally comes to terms with the way their body responds post-trauma, thriving anyway by integrating the moments of trauma and assigning language and meaning to the experience, while being truly heard in all the intensity of their narrative. I will discuss this more in chapter 3.

The Result of Trauma on the Inner Life of the Victim

After experiencing trauma, the person is left with changes in their inner experience of the world in addition to the body's alterations. I describe these changes in terms of shame, self-doubt, confusion, isolation, objectification, and a loss of power and control.

1. Shame

Violence tends to create a feeling of shame in the victim. Often victims begin to blame themselves for everything that goes wrong. Herman speaks of this in terms of guilt. She says the experience of violence "produces" an effect where "it is the victims, not the perpetrators, who feel guilty."[22] The shame and blame are passed to the victim instead of the one perpetrating violence.

Herman believes this is an attempt by victims to regain control. She says, "Guilt may be understood as an attempt to draw some useful lesson from disaster and to regain some sense of power and control," because imagining "that one could have done better may be more tolerable than to face the reality of utter helplessness."[23] In other words, victims' sense of guilt often stems from an attempt to believe they could have made a difference when no action was, in fact, imaginable. This guilt feeling

---

22 Herman, 53.
23 Herman, 53–54.

is a trick of the mind designed to help victims cope with overwhelming experiences in which they lacked autonomy.

Although this experience of guilt represents an attempt to understand, it quite often holds victims back from participating in life fully. The victim tries to regain control of a situation where they have no power by blaming themselves. Because logically, if they are to blame for the problems, then it is in their power to fix the situation. Unfortunately, it cannot be fixed with this false sense of control, and the result is that victims feel a sense of failure when they cannot repair things.

Part of the healing process for trauma experienced in violence involves replacing this previous coping mechanism (of accepting blame) to releasing oneself of responsibility. If the survivor of violence is to let go of this perceived obligation to accept fault, they must understand that nothing could have been done to change the outcome of what happened to them. Violence is traumatic because a person is harmed and unable to employ mechanisms for exerting agency.

This notion of letting go of responsibility often goes against the relationship advice offered by well-meaning people. Thus I argue we must shift how we hold victims accountable. When dealing with survivors of the trauma of violence, accountability does not mean we ask them to take responsibility for their actions. Instead, we hold victims accountable by helping them release obligation for taking on blame.

Brené Brown, a popular author and professor who is most known for her TED Talk and research in vulnerability, works to define shame in a way that enhances Herman's original thoughts. Although Brown also connects shame to concepts of embarrassment, guilt, and humiliation, she then draws a distinct line between shame and guilt.[24] She claims that "guilt is probably the

---

24 Brené Brown, *I Thought It Was Just Me (but It Isn't): Telling the Truth about Perfection, Inadequacy and Power* (New York: Gotham, 2007), 12.

term most often confused with shame" since "guilt and shame are both emotions of self-evaluation," but this is where the similarities end.[25] This is because "shame is about who we are and guilt is about behaviors that violate our values," a difference between "I am bad" and "I did something bad."[26] This is a critical distinction for understanding the experience of violence, since shame is an ontological category that involves one's understanding of themselves and who they are. Guilt is more of a disappointment in one's own controllable moral actions.

Violence, by its very nature, is something that happens to a person, outside of their autonomy and control. Victims should not feel guilty. Shame, however, is a deeply held pain based in a belief that a person is disgusting and unworthy of love. If I see myself as "bad" because of violence that happens to me (that I cannot change or regulate), this is very different from doing something "bad" by my own choice. This line of thinking leads us to see that victims of violence feel shame based on what the abuser imposes on them when their behavior does not line up with intensely high expectations. When a victim attempts to gain control by blaming themselves, it is based not in guilt, but in shame.

Shame is more a feeling of being afraid that if the person's deepest humanity is revealed, they are not worthy,[27] because when a victim of violence feels shame, they perceive an intense "fear of disconnection."[28] Thus a victim feels shame about who they are in response to the actions done to them. The internal experience after violence is one not of guilt but of shame. The victim is trapped with repeated messages that they are not worthy.

Shame is often a useful coping mechanism to survive in the moment. But healing, then, involves a shift in belief to realize we are humans worthy of love and connection. In other words, the

---

25 Brown, 13.
26 Brown, 13.
27 Brown, 12–17.
28 Brown, 20.

survivor believes they *are* good and not the person their abuser or perpetrator painted them to be.

It is our responsibility, as faith leaders, to help differentiate between shame and guilt in order to help survivors stop blaming themselves, as if they had a choice in the matter. It is also our responsibility to show survivors the opposite of shame and to shine light on their autonomy, power, and strength. This is how we can come along survivors of violence and make a valuable impact.

2. Self-Doubt

For victims of violence, feelings of self-doubt tend to be felt early on in the experience of chronic abuse. Walker describes this in terms of women underestimating "their ability to do anything" and doubting "their competence" as well as underplaying "any successes they had."[29] All too often I witness victims of violence doubting their ability to contribute anything positive to the world because of the constant criticism to which they are subjected in the experience of abuse. When a person is constantly made to feel as if they cannot meet absurdly high expectations, there tends also to be a false, and inadequate, understanding of their own self-worth and value.

In my own experience in working with trauma survivors, I see victims blame themselves for having made the choice to date a person who harms them, doubt they can ever find anyone else, and seem to lose the ability to stand up for themselves in situations in which, prior to chronic violence, they would have. The victim begins to lose their ability to trust their own ideas and thoughts. Perhaps the victim cooked a meal, and the abuser refuses to eat it. They do the laundry, and their abuser does not wear the clean clothes. They apply for the job and do not get it. When this kind of rejection happens repeatedly in many areas of life and chronically by someone they trust, a person begins to

---

29 Walker, *The Battered Woman*, 32.

believe they are worthless. The underlying messaging in their life is that nothing they do is good enough. They doubt themselves, unsure whether their own choices and actions are viable in the world. This adds another layer to the experience of violence. It becomes a habitual way of viewing the self in the world, making victims unsure whether they can impact the world for good.

As is true for shame, sometimes decades later a person is still trapped in this automatic response of self-doubt. But know that any one of us under this chronic disapproval and rejection, without consistent and healthy counterbalance, might also doubt ourselves. This is a normal response. Thus, we must be patient that even if a survivor is out of the violent relationship, they still might respond by doubting their own ability to make choices. This is because they are still reacting in the way violence trained them to respond.

Note that self-doubt is a normal human response to being treated as an object. When someone is treated as an object, instead of as a human, this often leads to self-doubt. Thus it is our responsibility as faith leaders to help restore opportunities for victims to believe in themselves again and counteract the feelings of self-doubt pushed on them by another person. We can do this by celebrating their autonomy, not excessively criticizing their choices we do not believe are good, and creating opportunities for success.

3. Confusion

Violence often leads to confusion as the person begins to live in their abuser's reality instead of their own. What do I mean by this? Often when a person is abused, when an abuser is creating another way of thinking about and behaving in the world, it is incredibly difficult for a victim to act within reality as it actually is.

For example, I hear women describing situations where items were thrown at them, their body felt the impact, and then the abuser claims they never did it. If the abuser is constantly undermining the victim's sense of what actually occurred, confusion is likely, even when the victim was there to experience the moment and saw it differently. Compound the situation with the perpetrator minimizing the victim's experience, exaggerating the victim's mistakes, minimizing their own actions, and everything else that makes up the experience of violence, and it is the recipe for feeling crazy and confused.

Lundy Bancroft, a leading psychologist in batterer intervention, writes about the notion that "confusion has been a part of the experience of almost every one of the hundreds of abused women" he has worked alongside.[30] He attributes this to several things: "either the abuser's manipulativeness, his popularity, or simply the mind-bending contrast between professions of love and his violence."[31] Under these three circumstances, certainty about what is real becomes harder to claim. The victim wonders if they are really loved, when the actions of the abuser say otherwise. The victim begins to question themselves when the abuser is popular and well loved. The victim becomes confused as to what is real and what is not.

In fact, often the most confusing question becomes: Who can I trust? Because what is really being asked is: Can I trust others' perceptions of my abuser? Can I trust my own actions? Can I trust my abuser? All of these questions, and their experience of how another person explains reality, can create feelings of deep confusion for a person experiencing violence.

4. Isolation

Violence tends to create distance between a victim and communal and social connections, whether intentional on the part of the abuser or not. Often the perpetrator will cut off the victim's

---

30 Lundy Bancroft, *Why Does He Do That? Inside the Minds of Angry and Controlling Men* (New York: Berkley, 2002), 77.
31 Bancroft, 77.

relationships with others or separate them from their family and friends in obvious ways. But sometimes the isolation happens indirectly as the victim pulls away and isolates themselves in order to avoid knowledge of the situation leaking out to others.

In some situations, it is obvious that the abuser is pulling the victim away. Bancroft describes, for example, seeing abusers drop "little" negative comments about the victim's family to slowly pull them away. He has seen abusers demand the victims' focus be on them, at the expense of family and friends, and he has watched abusers pressure the victim to "spend more time with him or to quit" their job.[32] All of these are examples of blatant isolation tactics.

The experience of isolation is a crucial piece of the internal experience after trauma, because humans usually desire connection and relationships. Brené Brown speaks of this desire in terms of humans being "biologically, emotionally, socially, and cognitively wired for connection."[33] We need connection, biologically, for survival. Thus, when the victim is pulled away from connections, which we biologically need to survive, the internal experience of the person is seriously affected. Victims need validation to know they are not crazy and others to verify that their perception of reality is correct, but if they are cut off from everyone but the perpetrator, what else can they possibly believe? They no longer have connections with people who treat them as human beings. They are isolated into an objectified experience.

5. Objectification

Pamela Cooper-White, former executive director of a network for battered women and currently a professor of psychology and religion at Union Theological Seminary, refers to Martin Buber's theory of "I-Thou" to explain this disconnection and objectification

---

32 Bancroft, 117.
33 Brown, *I Thought It Was Just Me (but It Isn't)*, 20.

that comes from violence. In an "I-Thou" relationship, people "yearn for mutuality and unmediated connection."[34] If I am an "I" and you are a "Thou," there is an innate and biological need for my "I" to connect with your "Thou." The point is that an "I" has a strong need to connect with another person's "Thou."[35] Cooper-White argues that violence is a complete "annihilation of connectivity" and a "dulling" of "human relationally through objectification."[36] It is not an "I-Thou" relationship. Instead, the "Thou" becomes an object. The victim becomes an "It." In other words, when a person becomes violent, the other is robbed of humanity and becomes an "It." This means that in the moments of violence, the perpetrator "chooses . . . to view another living being as an It rather than a Thou."[37]

Cooper-White reminds us it is a "common belief" that somehow the abuser "momentarily loses" his or her "head," but this is not true. Rather, "the abuser makes a critical shift in perspective,

---

34 Pamela Cooper-White, *The Cry of Tamar: Violence against Women and the Church's Response* (Minneapolis: Fortress, 2012), 41.

35 Martin Buber, *I and Thou*, trans. Walter Kaufmann (New York: Simon and Schuster, 1970). According to Kaufmann's prologue, Buber describes five different attitudes of a You: "I-I, I-It, It-It, We-We, and Us-Them" (14) and expands to an understanding of an "I-You" or "I-Thou" (14). Buber himself says, "The basic word I-You can only be spoken with one's whole being," and "The basic word I-It can never be spoken with one's whole being" (54); and, most important, "The basic word I-You establishes the world of relation" (56) for it is here one relates and connects to other human beings. Experiencing another is crucial because "as soon as we touch a You, we are touched by a breath of eternal life" (113). Within a marriage relationship, Buber believes, "two human beings reveal the You to one another" (95). And an I-It becomes toxic when a person "lets it have its way, the relentlessly growing It-world grows over him like weeds, his own I loses its actuality, until the incubus over him and the phantom inside him exchange the whispered confession of their need for redemption" (96).

36 Cooper-White, *The Cry of Tamar*, 41.

37 Cooper-White, 42.

no longer seeing" the victim "as a human being, equally precious" but instead "only as an object to be manipulated."[38] The abuser shifts from an "I-Thou" relationship to an "I-It" relationship with the victim. Or perhaps even an "It-It" relationship because, as I often point out, at what point do we lose our own humanity when we objectify others?

Abusers choose to treat a person as an object that can be controlled, kept from family, isolated from friends, asked to quit a job, and so forth. In the context of violence, being objectified without validation of humanity and proper relation to the "Thou," isolates the victim. When this is the only relationship a person regularly experiences, it can become nearly impossible to behave and function in any normal sense. We need community and interaction with other humans, a "Thou," to thrive.

6. Loss of Power and Control

In a violent situation, the victim, because it is in the nature of violence to take away a person's agency, lacks the ability to exert control or power. This is the most basic and obvious experience in all cases of abuse. James Newton Poling, former professor of pastoral theology, care, and counseling at Garrett-Evangelical Theological Seminary, defines the use of power as "the ability to act in effective ways with objects and people that make up our perceived world."[39] When persons experience physical, emotional, and/or sexual violence, their ability to actively seek what they desire is compromised. They no longer have control over acting in effective ways. Poling adds that abusers use "violence" as a "way of enforcing their power."[40]

The perpetrator moves to establish power and control over objects (as well as the people they treat as objects) with the use

---

38 Cooper-White, 42.
39 James Newton Poling, *The Abuse of Power: A Theological Problem* (Nashville: Abington, 1991), 24.
40 Poling, 69.

of violence. This stems from this distorted relationship of an "I-It" versus an "I-Thou" mode of relating. When one person treats another as an object, the victim's sense of self is lost, and a sense of control over outcomes is lost. Objects do not have control. An "It" does not get the ability to exert control. Only a "Thou" has control over acting in effective ways.

Poling describes this in concrete terms by allowing Karen, a survivor of sexual violence, to tell her own story. She says sexual violence is "not about sex"; instead, it is "about power and control. It's about big people over little people, superior over subordinate."[41] The perpetrator of violence dominates another. It is about oppression and using control over another.

The bottom line is that in the internal experience of violence, victims are made to feel powerless because of the actions of another. Perpetrators control activities that happen. They control feelings by manipulating the victim's entire environment. They control the victim's belief in their self-worth with continual negative messages. They effectively objectify a person (a "Thou") into an "It."

Understanding these six internal experiences of violence should help us, as faith leaders, to empathize with all the complexities of what it is like to be a victim of domestic violence or sexual assault. It is confusing, isolating, objectifying, and shaming; it creates feelings of self-doubt and makes one feel powerless to effect change. Truly, this internal experience of violence is a recipe for behaviors that might look different from what we think of as "normal" but, given the whole picture, are completely normal and expected.

Basic Definitions

Below are other basic definitions to help develop a framework for understanding the experience of a survivor of domestic violence and sexual assault with definitions and explanations.

---

41 Poling, 40.

ABUSE

Abuse includes any continual series of actions, words, or innuendoes that devalue the humanity of a person through power and control. In other words, abuse is the dehumanization of a person. The key to this definition is that abuse is about power and control over another, it is cyclical, and it tends to happen in patterns. This definition also gives clues into how we can tell the difference between who is the abuser and who is the victim. Ask yourself:

- Who holds the power?
- Who feels objectified?
- Who has a choice in their behavior?
- Who is angry about not controlling their life?
- Who uses attacking words (e.g., "You are a liar") in spaces where the two are alone?
- If one of the persons told the other not to go to work (see family, go to the store, etc.), which one of them obeys? Which would do what they want anyway?

It is important to differentiate between a one-time incident and abuse. Abuse is chronic and cyclical, which are not characteristics of one-time incidents. For example, an explosive incident where heated words are used is not verbal abuse. Abuse is when explosive words are used to control the person, continuously, over time.

This is an important distinction for how we respond appropriately. Chronic abuse requires a different response than does an incident that is over and done (such as a car accident or a one-time fight). Both might be traumatic, but abuse's chronic nature changes everything for survivors because it changes the body and the way we perceive ourselves in the world.

There are different kinds of abuse and different ways a person can be abused. One of these is emotional abuse.

Emotional Abuse

Emotional abuse is using any means necessary to control another person while evoking emotional agony. According to the Domestic Violence Hotline's resource, compiled by Dr. K. J. Wilson, an advocate, survivor, and professor, emotional abuse is "any use of words, voice, action, or lack of action meant to control, hurt, or demean another person."[42]

In my experience working with survivors, I often hear, "I wish he'd hit me so I could say, 'Look here, he did this to me,'" because if this is true, there would be a mark, a physical indication of violence to watch heal. When nothing is visible, it is easier than one might think to doubt it ever happened. I make this claim from experience. Of the seventy-eight items listed in the Domestic Violence Sourcebook compiled by Safeplace and the National Domestic Violence Hotline (beyond extreme violence like murder, shooting, and stabbing), I have personally experienced fifty-three of those listed.[43] These fifty-three things happen to be instances that leave a person controlled but tend not to leave marks. I might be an intelligent, educated woman, but even I found it easier to believe it was not happening than to confront the horror that someone I loved, and who I believed loved me, was causing harm. When there is something to observe and point to, the survivor has something tangible to hold and process. But when the abuse is not so obvious and does not leave visible, tangible markings, it is hard to hold the reality of abuse in our awareness.

I hear survivors say things like:

- "When I secretly recorded one of our fights and listened to it later, I knew I wasn't crazy."

---

42 K. J. Wilson, *When Violence Begins at Home: A Comprehensive Guide to Understanding and Ending Domestic Abuse* (Alameda, CA: Hunter House, 2006), 11.
43 Wilson, 9–14.

- "When I walked by the shattered items and I could see it and point to it, I knew I was not imagining things."
- "When I wrote out what I was hearing so I could finally look at it objectively and think about what was happening, I became aware something was not right in our relationship."
- "When I heard myself saying things in therapy, I knew something was wrong."

In each of these four instances, the survivor was able to find something tangible to help them hold the reality of abuse in their awareness. This is important because emotional abuse often does not leave visible marks or damages, which makes processing the experience very difficult. This is one of the many reasons victims stay with their abusers. In situations such as this it can be difficult to pinpoint and know exactly what the problem is.

Because of the lack of obvious and overt violence, emotional abuse is often the part of violence causing the most agony. Bancroft claims that "even among women who have experienced violence from a partner, half or more report that the man's emotional abuse is what is causing them the greatest harm."[44] Why is this? Because emotional violence is incredibly complex and is detrimental to a person's well-being. It involves coercion, blame, and threats—accusations and critical comments. It is crafted from manipulation, and the abuser enforces direct influence on a person's ability to understand reality, so the person experiencing violence actually enters the abuser's reality in order to survive. Bancroft argues that even the victim's own "grievances" are "constantly turned around on her, so everything is her own fault."[45]

Therefore, building on Bancroft, I make this claim: emotional abuse is often experienced and perceived as worse than physical harm. Emotional abuse is a torment of the mind as well as a

---

44 Bancroft, *Why Does He Do That?*, 8.
45 Bancroft, 9.

manipulation of thoughts and perceived reality. When this happens, the victim often needs something tangible to hold onto (a recording, a broken item, written words, or something else) to process the difference between what is real and what their perpetrator demands they believe.

A true and accurate understanding of emotional violence is often just outside awareness. The victim knows they feel pain and their body responds to survive, but there tends to be difficulty making the knowledge of abuse a cognitive declaration. This is also why we cannot force people to leave their abusers or take action. Their primitive brains and their body's reaction might agree with you, but it may not be in active cognition yet. This awareness is something we can invest time in helping them see but certainly not demand from them. We must work with the body, not against it.

The logical conclusion of what I am saying is that all abuse is emotional abuse. For example, verbal abuse happens within the context of emotional abuse because verbal abuse changes the way a person views themselves. However, it is important to note that emotional abuse can occur without the use of words. A person can be free from verbal abuse and still be emotionally abused. Some violence involves such things as body language and attitudes that may or may not use words. The point is that every type of abuse is emotional abuse. Physical assault, sexual abuse, financial abuse—all are also manifestations of emotional abuse, using any means necessary to control another person in a way that damages emotional competency. Thus, I claim this "just" in the phrase I often hear, "It was just emotional abuse," is not true. Emotional abuse is devastating and needs to be taken seriously.

However, I must offer the disclaimer that of the hundreds of women I have walked with over the years, every single one of them who thought they were not physically abused but "*just* emotionally abused" or "*just* verbally assaulted" figured out in their healing process that they were indeed violated on a bodily level. Emotional abuse is tied to the body. In fact, I would say that emotional abuse is physical abuse because it changes the way the brain responds to stimuli and alters the body's chemistry. I will discuss this further in chapter 2.

Sexual Abuse

Sexual abuse involves any action, innuendo, or behavior that is forced or coerced without the continual and explicit consent of all partners. According to the Domestic Violence Hotline's resource, sexual abuse includes "any sexual behavior meant to control, manipulate, humiliate, or demean another person."[46]

Sexual abuse quite often involves submission, sometimes even a willing submission. What do I mean by this? Often a victim will "give in" and submit because it is easier to participate in what their abuser wants than it is to fight for what they want. But it is important to know that this is still sexual abuse, as it is a violation of intended response and manipulation of a victim's body and the person's will. Sometimes we see victims believing they were to blame because they "allowed it" or "gave into the pressure." However, I urge us to rethink this. When you participate in an activity to avoid further harm, this is not true consent. Unwilling submission does not equal consent to participate in a sexual activity.

Beyond this I argue that sexual abuse goes much deeper than the physical body's participation in sexual activity. Fundamentally, sexual violence is about the person's spirit and energy, because the sexual also involves the spiritual. Rob Bell, who traveled with Oprah Winfrey's "The Life You Want Tour," claims in his controversial work *Sex God* that "whether it's what we do with our energies or how we feel about our bodies or wanting to have the control in relationships . . . much of life is in some way connected

---

46 Wilson, *When Violence Begins at Home*, 13.

with our sexuality."[47] In other words, our lives are sexual whether we participate in sexual activities or not. "When we begin to sort through all of the issues surrounding our sexuality," he continues, "we quickly end up in the spiritual" because "Sex. God. They're connected. And they can't be separated. Where the one is, you will always find the other."[48]

As Bell so eloquently points out: "You can't talk about sexuality without talking about how we are made. And that will inevitably lead to who made us."[49] Thus, we tend to naturally and logically think of the divine and the spiritual when we think of the sexual.

This is important. The sexual and spiritual are interconnected. When we talk about the sexual, we are also speaking of the spiritual. They are connected and cannot be separated. Our bodies are who we are, as Elisabeth Moltmann-Wendel reveals in her book *I Am My Body*.[50] We are ontologically connected to our bodies. Thus, in a real sense, sexual abuse is spiritual abuse. When we talk about the violation of the body (as with any other type of abuse), there also needs to be talk about a violation of the person's very spirit or ontological being. The violation of consent on a bodily level is a violation of consent of a person's very spirit. We are whole creatures: body, mind, spirit, and relational. When the body is violated, so also is the spiritual breath violated.

PHYSICAL ABUSE

Physical abuse is any behavior, innuendo, or activity used to control the location, movement, or direction of another person's body without their agency or consent. According to the Domestic

---

47 Rob Bell, *Sex God: Exploring the Endless Connections between Sexuality and Spirituality* (Grand Rapids, MI: Zondervan, 2007), 13.

48 Bell, 14–15.

49 Bell, 15.

50 Elisabeth Moltmann-Wendel, *I Am My Body: A Theology of Embodiment* (New York: Continuum, 1995).

Violence Hotline's resource, "physical abuse is any use of size, strength, or presence to hurt or control someone else."[51]

Unfortunately, it seems to be a common belief that physical abuse constitutes body-to-body contact. The assumption is, for a person to be physically abused, one body must touch another body. However, physical abuse includes anything that involves the body, whether or not there is direct bodily contact with the abuser.

In other words, throwing objects, blocking a person's body in a room, keeping someone trapped in a car, forcing someone to stay awake are all examples of physical abuse, even though it is entirely possible the abuser never makes physical contact with the victim's body. The assumption that physical abuse is limited to being punched, kicked, or shot must be put aside. We must learn to expand the categorization of physical abuse because this will help us respond to domestic violence and sexual assault in better, healthier ways.

Physical abuse includes the claim, "They hit me," but it also goes beyond to, "I was trapped," "I didn't feel safe," or "My body felt violated." Physical abuse is anything that involves the victim's physical body, whether it was touched by the perpetrator or not.

Again, I would even go so far as to say that all abuse is physical abuse because, by its very nature, abuse affects one's brain, nervous system, and entire physiological being. Chronic emotional abuse affects the way the brain learns to respond to situations and stimuli. Verbal abuse creates a habitual response in the body. Thus, I argue that all abuse, whether a person is touched or not, is physical abuse.

AGENCY

Agency is the ability to exert influence and choice over what happens next. In the experience of violence, a person's agency is

---

51 Wilson, *When Violence Begins at Home,* 9.

completely violated. What makes abuse and violence truly traumatizing are those moments where a person cannot actively choose or participate (either positively or negatively) in what is happening. Instead, the experience happens to a person who has no ability to act.

In order for us to respond to persons who have felt the experience of having their agency and choice violated, we must find ways to give people back their choices. What victims of violence need is the ability to exert their own influence and power of choice over what happens in their life. Survivors need ways to exert agency.

I will return here to the story that began this chapter. I was so proud of the woman in that narrative. She took her power back against all odds. She walked miles after a physical assault to get what she needed. I celebrated that strength. I praised her for being so strong, even though two very powerful influences in her life (her partner and her faith community) were trying to take her agency and choice away. This is how we must respond to the knowledge of domestic violence and sexual assault in our faith communities. As people who care about victims of violence, we must celebrate their power and strength, believing that victims know what they need, even if it does not make sense to us, and letting them have control of their own lives. When we choose to respond to survivors of violence in this way, we empower them with the experience of their own agency and freedom. When we determine what is best for a survivor and limit the control they have over their own life, we are no better than their perpetrators controlling their life. Instead, we must honor and highlight the beautiful human agency survivors exhibit every day.

AUTONOMY

This term speaks to the freedom to be and to act. Autonomy is about gathering up your initiative to exert your agency and manage yourself. Autonomy involves the strength to grasp hold of your own power and control to make choices you desire. When we respond to disclosures of domestic violence or sexual assault, we must keep in mind these notions of autonomy. The concept of autonomy is closely connected to agency, and the terms are often used interchangeably.

I had a mother come to me one day in complete devastation. She had just learned her daughter had been sexually assaulted and had no idea how she could help. I told her the most valuable thing she could do was to find ways to help her daughter regain her autonomy and her sense of power and control over her own choices. When a survivor comes to you disclosing violence, ask yourself these questions: How can you give them the tools to exert their agency and choice? How can you empower them to find access to the control of their own ability to make choices again? Or, as I used to pose the problem to my college students, "How can you give someone the tools to save themselves?" It is important to understand this concept fully. We do not *save* victims of violence. We are not the heroes and heroines. We are simply present and creating opportunities for survivors to fully thrive. The survivors are the heroes and heroines of their own story. They deserve the credit and honor for surviving and thriving.

CONSENT

Consent is an ongoing, enthusiastic, and continual *yes* throughout all parts of a sexual experience. As I often tell survivors, required or expected consent *is not* consent. Consent is an ongoing, enthusiastic, continual, and active participation in an activity. There are many ways consent can be violated:

- if a person agrees to one thing but not the next
- if a person wants to do something to get it over with
- if a person is afraid to say no (or says no)
- if a person is unable to say no (perhaps due to being unconscious or ill)

This means that even in committed relationships, one could violate their partner's consent. This also means that if fear is present, there is no consent. It is incredibly difficult to do what is best for you and choose what you really want when you feel dread and anxiety.

Crisis

A crisis is an intense situation where a person can recover quickly and employ mechanisms to adequately cope with the issue. This might include various engagement strategies of fighting or running, or it might include the actions of various social strategies. The distinguishable difference between crisis and trauma is that in crisis, a person can employ strategies for survival, whereas in trauma, they are unable to act in ways that make a difference.

Dehumanization

To dehumanize someone is to attempt to take away the sense of humanity from another person and reduce them to an object. The word *dehumanize* is synonymous with "objectify." When a person is dehumanized in the experience of violence, it is as if their perpetrator is demanding they lose their sense of purpose, meaning, and basic humanity. They go from an active agent to being treated as someone's passive object. The person abusing them treats them as a "thing" rather than a human, and when a person is chronically treated in this way, it affects how they behave. Truly any response and behavior a person has in response to objectification is completely normal and expected. To be deprived of your humanity tends to create extreme reactions and rightfully so.

For example, when a victim is thrown around in the same way a person might throw a stone into the lake or is kicked in the same way someone might kick a ball, we know the person has been reduced to the level of an object—in this case, a stone or ball. Thus, to throw a person as one would a stone or kick a person like a ball is a practice of dehumanization.[52] Dehumanization occurs when a human person is treated like an object. Being forced into this experience is truly horrible.

Because dehumanization is a characteristic of abuse, we often see survivors of violence intentionally exerting their power in a way that highlights their realness as humans. For example, they might make an active choice to use their body to feel the sexual experience in the way they desire. Or, they might do the exact opposite, refusing to use their body in the sexual experience. There are many other examples of how we often see victims of violence trying to feel more human than object. We might also see victims cutting themselves, consuming alcohol and drugs, and a vast array of other methods. In reality what they are doing is staking a claim to their humanity and control. This behavior is screaming, "I am human" (and possibly while numbing the painful effects of being dehumanized).

Instead of harshly chastising and judging these behaviors, we need to find ways to say we see the survivor's humanity and celebrate that reclaiming of power and choice. To affirm a survivor's power of autonomy does not mean we celebrate them causing harm to themselves (such as with cutting). It means we are affirming the very basis of why we are seeing these behaviors. It means we are affirming their beauty and worth as a human worthy of love and connection. I propose that when we truly affirm this basic human need for validation and dignity, the need for self-declarative behaviors (that are less than healthy) will tend to fade away.

If we truly comprehend this concept of dehumanization, then we understand these behaviors are often happening because victims desperately need to feel they are active beings with agency. We all have this need. This also means victim behavior is not an

---

52 The example I chose was overtly physical, but this does not mean dehumanization is always a physical action. A person can be dehumanized in any form of abuse.

indication that they are a sinful mess in need of our corrective response. Many of the behaviors we see in victims and survivors are actions that make sense to a person who is reclaiming autonomy and agency after dehumanization.

I believe that if we can learn to respond to dehumanization correctly, in ways that give survivors the feeling of choice and agency, we will be doing something positive for them and providing the very thing survivors are seeking in their behavioral response (that we have a tendency to judge). We can make a difference for survivors by putting aside judgments of their behavior and finding ways to help them feel their human agency.

In other words, many of the behaviors we see in victims after they are violated and dehumanized are often considered "sin" in the eyes of some church leaders and pastors. But I am encouraging us to think of many such behaviors not in terms of sin but as actions that demonstrate how the survivor is standing up with their own power and autonomy to declare their humanity in the world. This is an exciting thing to celebrate. These self-acknowledging behaviors are less "sin" and instead often the holiest action.

We cannot force survivors of violence to submit to an understanding of sin as simply a bad behavior. For survivors of violence, a "bad behavior" could be a sign the person is claiming their agency after someone tried to take it away. In other words, when it comes to an oppressed people who are dehumanized and violated, we must think about our theology differently.

Violence is dehumanizing, an attempt at robbing the person of a feeling of being human. People need to have agency and autonomy regarding their own bodies and emotions and will go to great lengths to feel their basic ontological humanity, especially when chronically abused. It is important to realize these behaviors are normal human responses to being dehumanized. In my experience, if we give survivors some time and space without judgment, while simultaneously affirming their value and dignity, they will be free to heal; and we will be able to watch as they become empowered, thriving persons who effect positive change.

DOMESTIC VIOLENCE

Domestic violence is usually understood in the context of an intimate partner relationship but technically includes anyone in the household. When speaking of intimate partners, domestic violence involves one partner exerting power and control over the other in order to control the outcome of activities or events. This control objectifies the victim, and rather than being treated as a human, the person's agency is stripped away. The partner without control can no longer make all choices about what happens next without considering every demand, desire, or wish of their partner.

FAMILY VIOLENCE

Family violence happens in the context of the family unit or persons who live together.

POWER AND CONTROL WHEEL

Several years ago in Duluth, Minnesota, a radical new way to view domestic violence emerged. We call it the "Power and Control Wheel." In a recent criminal case, the prosecutor's office called on me as an expert witness. I was asked to testify about the Power and Control Wheel. After I was sworn in by the judge, our assistant district attorney asked me to explain what role power and control played in an abusive relationship. The members of the jury seemed eager to hear what I had to say, and I explained the importance of the Power and Control Wheel. I started with the story of how and why it was designed. I had talked for about twenty seconds when the defense attorney declared that the history of the wheel was extraneous and unimportant. Unfortunately, the judge sustained his complaint; and the jury never got to hear the full story of how survivors of violence, and the researchers who listened to their stories, were the ones who had created this tool. I think that is an important piece. The wheel comes from the voices of those who experienced violence and is a great example of a tool that is survivor informed.

Ellen Pence, the matriarch of the Duluth Model and an amazing contributor to the field of domestic violence before her death in 2012, sat down with women who were abused and began to identify where their stories were similar. As the survivors told their experiences of being controlled by their abusers, they gathered together different categories and organized them in the shape of a wheel.[53] When their stories held something in common, they put it in the wheel.

The wheel is divided into eight sections: Using Coercion and Threats; Using Intimidation; Using Emotional Abuse; Using Isolation; Minimizing/Denying/Blaming; Using Children; and Using Male Privilege (which we usually translate as "Using Entitlement/Privilege" to include all genders); and Using Economic Abuse. Inside these eight categories is the center of it all, power and control; and around the outside of the wheel it reads "Physical Violence and Sexual Violence." This wheel is now widely accepted in the field as a tool to identify the complex nature of abuse, especially in the context of intimate partners.

Thankfully, even though I could not share with the jury the valuable information that the wheel was created from the narrative of actual survivors, the judge did allow me to explain the wheel and offer guidance on how this informs our understanding of the role of power and control in an abusive relationship. The jury listened intently as I explained how the wheel reveals the ways we often see perpetrators employing various tactics to exert power and control over their victim.

---

53 To see Ellen Pence talk about designing the wheel, see www.youtube
   .com/watch?v=r9dZOgr78eE.

I began to describe each slice of the wheel, offered the main point of the tactic, and then listed some real-life examples. Although I was simply testifying as an expert and had no knowledge of the case, I hoped some of what I would say could apply to the current criminal case.

My explanation to the jury went something like this as I went around each of the slice on the wheel and identified the key point of the tactic and offered a few examples.

1. *Tactic: Using Coercion and Threats.* The point of this tactic is to send a message to the victim that they will be harmed if they do not comply with what the abuser wants. The victim is forced into a behavior or action to avoid something worse. Examples include such things as the abuser threatening

    *   to take away the children.
    *   to file paperwork identifying them as an unfit parent.
    *   to have an affair.
    *   that if they go to jail, they are harming their own child.
    *   to cause harm to their family, hurt pets, or slash their tires.

2. *Tactic: Using Intimidation.* The point of this tactic on the Power and Control Wheel is to instill fear in the person being abused. The perpetrator pushes a victim into a particular behavior or action to avoid harm. Examples include such things as the abuser

    *   revealing a weapon or claiming they have access to one.
    *   using their body to tower over the victim.
    *   making various threats.

3. *Tactic: Using Emotional Abuse.* The point of this tactic is to tear down the victim's sense of self-worth and power. As the person hears again and again that they are worthless, it depletes their sense of self-worth. Examples:

    - Calling the victim names
    - Using verbal language or body language to attack the victim's body image
    - Rejecting everything they say, do, or create

4. *Tactic: Using Isolation.* The point of this slice of the Power and Control Wheel is to pull the victim away from their support system. If a victim is separated from parents, friends, or other persons who can support them, it is easier for the abuser to exert control. It is also more difficult for the survivor to think clearly about who they are and who they can be. Examples:

    - Not wanting the victim to spend too much time away
    - Claiming that as a couple the victim and abuser need to stand together—"it's us against the world"
    - Not approving of the victim's choices of friends
    - Claiming to "love" the victim so much they should stay at home with them instead of going to spend time with another person

5. *Tactic: Minimizing, Denying, and Blaming.* The point of this tactic is to prove that whatever the abuser did was not a big deal and anything that was done by the victim is a problem, which the abuser hugely exaggerates. In this clever tactic, the victim is made to feel like the one who is the abuser. Examples:

    - Saying things like, "It was only a shove, not a punch."

- Telling the victim, "You know how to push my buttons. You shouldn't have done that," or "If you would have just done *x*, I wouldn't have had to do this."
- After they do something drastic and devastating, saying something like, "I left my job for you. You made me sacrifice so much and you never let me do *x*." It shifts the focus off of what the abuser did, minimizing it, and overemphasizes the actions of the victim.

6. *Tactic: Using Children.* The point of this tactic is to get the victim to bend to the abuser's will for the sake of the children or other significant persons (such as friends or family). This is often the soft spot a perpetrator can easily use to control the victim. Examples include such things as:

- Using the children to relay messages instead of talking directly to the victim, "Tell your mother this meal is disgusting. Who wants to go out for pizza?"
- Manipulating the situation to make the victim feel as if everything they did (and not the abuser's action) affected the child. The abuser claims that it is the victim's fault the child is suffering. For example: "Look at little Joey. You say you want to leave me. Do you see how distraught you are making him?"

7. *Tactic: Using Male Privilege (or Entitlement and Privilege in General).* In this tactic, the abusers actually believe they are entitled to get what they want. They believe they have the right to act a certain way because they are entitled to something. Abusers tend not to think they are doing something wrong. They believe they have a reason

to behave the way they do. They are convinced they are entitled to act a certain way. Examples:

- Abuser takes all paychecks—saying all money in the family is theirs
- Abuser demands sexual relations because they "deserve it"
- Abuser insists it is impossible to experience rape in a marriage (or committed partnership)

8. *Tactic: Using Economic Abuse.* The point of this tactic is to control all financial income and spending. One of the most essential components of basic survival is having access to financial resources. If this is cut off, the victim is left without sufficient means to stand alone or survive without their abuser. Examples:

- Making the victim account for all spending (even explain items on a receipt)
- Making the victim ask permission for money (whether it is the victim's own money or a joint account)
- Insisting that all financial decisions go through one person

When I finished this explanation of the Power and Control Wheel, the jury seemed disturbed. Suddenly I made it easy for them to imagine why a victim would act a little odd. Anyone dealing with this situation might act a little strangely. After the prosecution questioned me, it was the defense attorney's turn. Of course, he attacked everything about me. He made fun of the fact that I worked on fundraising campaigns, because how could I possibly know anything about violence (never mind the fact they were fundraisers *for* victim services). But, eventually, when none of his attacks worked, he tried to make the wheel seem unimportant by calling it "that wheel thing" in a sarcastic tone. Despite his best efforts, the Power and Control Wheel remained a powerful tool for the prosecution because it helped the jury begin to understand the complexities of intimate partner violence.

As the trial continued, I learned quickly that I had been called to the stand because the victim was testifying on behalf of the defense. She claimed that everything she originally reported was false and that she had caused all the damage to herself. The prosecutor's office brought me in to say this is completely normal behavior from a victim who is caught in the slices of the Power and Control Wheel.

I would argue that not only was her behavior completely normal but it is also entirely expected. When I was called to the stand a second time (knowing more details of the case), I argued her behavior served as proof to me she was a victim of intimate partner violence. I expect this kind of behavior from those who are manipulated and controlled.

Why am I telling this story in a book for pastors, Christian caregivers, counselors, and religious professionals? Because as much as I want juries to understand the complexities of domestic violence and sexual assault, I also want faith leaders to know this. Abuse is so much more than being smacked around, shot, and stabbed. An abuser can use the fear and threat of being harmed, which is often much more powerful and involves less of a need to use physical force. The wheel offers a glimpse into the whole picture of domestic abuse and not just the black eyes. It explains why victims exhibit weird behaviors or withdraw their accusations. The wheel is a useful tool to begin to understand the horror of living under the power and control of another person.

When a person is chronically abused in the ways we see in the wheel, at the hands of their intimate partner, it damages the body, mind, and spirit. It causes behaviors that seem paradoxical, at least when we do not know the whole experience.

Again, I expect the behavior of victims caught in cycles of power and control to be erratic, inconsistent, and seemingly paradoxical. This tends to serve as proof that they are victims.

SECONDARY VICTIM

This phrase is used to identify those who experience trauma secondhand. In other words, they observe and witness the abuse but do not experience it as the primary victim. Often secondary victims are the children of the person being abused or other persons who live under the care of the victim or perpetrator. Generally, a "secondary victim" is understood to be someone affected by the primary aggression but not harmed directly.

SEXUAL ASSAULT

Sexual assault is any action, innuendo, or behavior that is forced or coerced without the continual and explicit consent of all parties involved in the intimate encounter. Consent is an ongoing and consistent yes; everything else means no. Again, note: It is possible for a person to verbally or physically appear to consent to a sexual act in order to avoid further harm, but that *is not* consent. Consent requires enthusiastic and continual active participation.

It is important to remember that when a person's consent is disregarded, they lose the ability to control what happens next. In those moments, one person lacks the ability to influence what is happening to them. That person is no longer participating in the experience as an agent of their own body; instead, the sexual act happens to them. Sexual assault involves, at its most basic explanation, a loss of bodily agency at the hands of another person.

SURVIVOR CENTERED

To be survivor centered is to always consider the needs of the person who experienced violence and to be informed by their voice and perspective. When an individual or agency is survivor centered, this involves creating spaces designed for survivors, being aware of how you position your body to communicate, understanding how you approach the topic, and so much more. Being survivor centered is about putting the survivor in the center of your thoughts prior to any action or words.

A faith community could be survivor centered by considering the perspective of victims of violence before words are spoken. For example, if you are preaching on a difficult passage, think carefully about how it could be heard through the ears of a survivor of violence.

Trauma Informed

To be trauma informed is to respond to survivors in a way that considers the nature and complexity of the trauma experience. To respond to disclosures of violence in a trauma-informed manner is to reply in a way that reflects an understanding of the intricacies of trauma. This includes understanding the biology of trauma (see chapter 2); the aftermath of violence on a person; and at least a little knowledge of active listening, connecting to and understanding the speaker to reduce the potential for secondary trauma.

For example, it is trauma informed to ask permission to touch a survivor after sexual assault. This includes a simple hand to the shoulder. Touching can be incredibly retraumatizing for a person after the experience of violence. To be trauma informed is to be educated (informed) about trauma and respond accordingly.

Victim/Survivor

These two terms are often used simultaneously to describe the person who experienced abuse and violence. However, others use the term *victim* to mean the person who is still *in* the abuse and *survivor* to mean the person who is *out* of the experience of violence. The problem with the terms *victim* and *survivor* is they are often used to describe the lowly status of one person who was dominated by another. Thus, the important thing to remember about your word choice is that some people do not want to be known as a victim. Others do not want to be called a survivor. Listen to the cues of the person who is in the experience to determine what words you select.

Violence

Violence occurs when one person or group exerts power over another person in order to control the outcome of activities or events to the point that it dehumanizes, objectifies, and takes away a sense of agency. Violence is a key component of being abused by an intimate partner, in family violence, or in sexual assault.

Mainstream media often teaches that violence involves blood and guts. We see a warning about violence in a movie, and we know it means there might be weapons of some sort. We see a violence warning on a video game, and we know there might be some fighting and punching. However, violence is so much more than exposure to gruesome physical actions. It is the exertion of power and control over a person so they are unable to control their own life and choices. It might involve a weapon or words; or the person themselves might be the weapon.

Reference Guide: Ways a Person Can Be Abused and What You Might Hear

Physically: This form of abuse includes anything that involves the body (even what does not involve body-to-body contact). This could include everything from the use of weapons to throwing objects to preventing someone from leaving the room. You might hear things like:

- "They hit me."
- "I was trapped."
- "I didn't feel safe."
- "I lost control of my body."

Emotionally: This form of abuse includes attempts at manipulating another person's reality, coercion, blame, or making threats. Often there is nothing to point to and prove this is where the victim was hurt. You might hear things like:

- "I'm so stupid."
- "If I could just do better."
- "What is wrong with me?"

Sexually: This form of abuse can be blatantly obvious with force or more coercive. Often victims will give in or stop fighting, but this is no less of an assault. You might hear things like:

- "I feel disgusting."
- "I'm so embarrassed."
- "I need a shower."

Note: There are many other ways a person can be abused (verbally, socially, financially, technologically, legally, spiritually, and so forth). See recommended resources for further guidance.

Case Study: Why Won't She Just Leave?

Joan is a young, unmarried woman with two children: Alex, age two, and Annie, age six. Joan dated Sam for three years, on and off. During one of the "off" times, Joan became pregnant with Alex, who was born after she returned to Sam. Sam was not Annie's father, either.

Sam has never forgiven Joan for her other relationships, and every chance he gets, he reminds her how horrible she is for having a baby with another man. In his tirade of guilt trips, he fails to mention that Joan left because he punched her so hard that she had to miss work. She called in a week straight, waiting to return until she could see out of both her eyes again. In the three years Joan and Sam have been together, she's depended on him to provide housing for herself and her kids, and his paycheck usually buys Alex's diapers. When she leaves, it usually is not for long, because she cannot stand to see her baby in dirty diapers.

One time after Joan left Sam and wanted to make it on her own, she stood in the grocery store holding a box of tampons and a bag of diapers. She started sobbing, right there, because the ten dollars she had to her name would not buy both. Someone she knew from church walked by and looked at her as if she were crazy. Since then she has refused to be anywhere near a church; she is too humiliated. Joan feels Sam's hate for her when she is with him and feels humiliated when she is near a church congregation. She is isolated and alone.

You are the pastor. One day, when you are pumping gas, you look up to see Joan in the next car over. She puts her head down, but you say hi anyway. She lifts her head, and you see that it looks like she's been crying for days and there are ligature marks on her neck. The kids are in the back seat seemingly oblivious. As you approach her for further conversation you notice she's only put five dollars' worth of gas in her tank. There are a few conclusions you can draw from such a small amount. What would you do?

Consider this additional information one item at a time:

1. Death potential

    •   Leaving is the most dangerous time. If she dies, who takes care of her kids?
    •   Ligature marks are indicative of strangulation. It takes only four pounds of pressure to kill a person by strangulation.[54]

---

54 For more information about strangulation (including signs, symptoms, and how to help, access the Strangulation Training Institute. Their website notes: "The force needed to strangle someone is considerably less than many might assume. It can take about 4.4 psi for 10–30 seconds to strangle someone into unconsciousness if they have blocked off the jugular vein, Berkowitz said during her presentation, while it takes 11

2. Finances
   - He helps pay for diapers for the baby.
   - He provides shelter.

3. Stability
   - Leaving any relationship when you live together is difficult.
   - Leaving would be a significant change in location, income, and general stability.

4. Self-blame
   - She loves Sam and believes that if she could just do things right, he wouldn't hurt her. She believes that it's all her fault.
   - She has zero confidence in her ability to survive on her own.

5. Love
   - She loves Sam. Sometimes he makes her laugh so hard she can't breathe. Those are the best days of her life.
   - Even though Alex and Annie aren't Sam's kids, he treats them pretty well. She loves him for that, even though he treats her badly.

6. Humiliation
   - If she leaves again, at some point she's going to find herself in the store crying over tampons and diapers.
   - If she lives in a shelter, she will be officially labeled homeless.

psi for 10–20 seconds to block the carotid arteries and cause someone to fall unconscious." See www.strangulationtraininginstitute.com/authorities-lead-strangulation-investigation-training/ (accessed June 7, 2018).

7. Survival Expert

- You might think the best course of action is to get her out, but maybe she knows that if she leaves for good, Sam's anger will escalate, and he will probably attempt to kill her. Last time she left he had his hands around her neck so long she passed out. She wants to avoid that at all costs.

2

Understanding the Brain and Body in Trauma

I was working as an employee of the Kansas Coalition Against Sexual and Domestic Violence (KCSDV) when I saw one of our trainers use a fascinating technique that changed how I view trauma. I still enjoy utilizing this activity in a group exercise we call the "Trauma Lens,"[1] because it always helps audiences who are trying to understand the experience of a survivor of violence to think outside of their expectations.

The Trauma Lens activity consists of three parts.

1. First, the leader guides the group to list all the emotions they can imagine are felt by a person who has experienced domestic violence and sexual assault. The group members tend to list things like:

   - Sadness
   - Shame
   - Confusion
   - Being overwhelmed

---

1 This Trauma Lens is used by the Kansas Coalition Against Sexual and Domestic Violence in training sessions. When I worked as a cotrainer on vicarious trauma, victim services, allies and advocate training, and so forth, the Trauma Lens was utilized on many occasions.

- Grief
- Anger
- Fear
- Feeling numb

These are all completely normal responses to the traumatic experience of having another person violate the body and mind.

2. Second, the group is asked to list what behaviors are common as responses to these strong emotions. For example:

- If they say "anger," I challenge them to consider what behavior is normal for this emotion (perhaps verbal aggression would constitute an understandable response to this emotion).
- If they say "overwhelming grief," I prompt them to consider what behavior would logically follow (perhaps choosing drugs or alcohol to numb, or selecting an action that reveals an inability to enforce boundaries would seem like reasonable behaviors in response to the extreme emotions felt in violence).

When I lead this exercise, I want the people in my audience to consider the possibility that a wide range of behavioral actions is normal and directly linked to the person's strong emotions following the violation of violence.

3. Finally, the group is asked to consider how society would respond to these behaviors. I challenge the audience to really analyze what we say when we see these behaviors in our spaces. For example:

- If the participants say a common behavior is "hypersexuality," perhaps the societal response might be, "She's a slut."

- If the behavior is "verbal aggression," a typical response is, "They're so angry!"
- If they list the behavior of "isolation," an average response is, "They are crazy. They need meds."
- If we see the behavior from a victim who appears to lack boundaries, we often say, "They have issues."
- If we observe defiant and hostile behavior, we might react by dropping access to whatever services or assistance we can provide.
- If we watch survivors get into more bad situations, we blame them.
- If we hear that a victim has caused harm to themselves, it is not unusual for society to claim they are just sick and/or crazy.

With this third question, the audience begins to see the connection between the behavioral response to trauma and their own responses. My goal is to help people understand that victims have perfectly valid emotional responses to their trauma, and all too often we call the normal responses to violence a problem. By so doing, we inhibit our ability to respond to victims in a trauma-informed way.

When a person is violated by their intimate partner or someone they trusted, it creates extreme emotions like anger, sadness, shame, and shock. Those emotions come with certain expected behaviors. Those behaviors tend to be judged harshly by secular society and even the church. But, most significantly, these judgments lead to retraumatization for an already traumatized group of people.

Try this activity out for yourself:

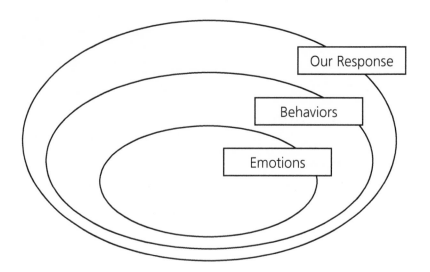

The Trauma Lens

1. List the emotions of a person who has experienced domestic violence and sexual assault.
2. List what behaviors are common because of these emotions.
3. List typical responses to these behaviors.

After the exercise, my question is always the same: So, what can we do? What is the variable that can be addressed in a particular situation?

- Can we address how victims feel in response to violence? No, that would probably be as difficult as controlling the violence itself.
- Can we control how victims behave in response to those emotions? No, that is not in our control.
- The only thing we can change and control is ourselves and our response. The variable we can shift is that victims receive harsh judgments by us and even from well-intentioned church leaders.

When we understand what is happening with victims' bodies, seemingly odd behaviors make sense. In fact, our bodies were designed to respond to trauma in these seemingly paradoxical ways in order to survive. Although there are many ways to think about the body's response to trauma, I help professionals understand three basic ways to explain how our brain is working to keep us alive when we are traumatized. These are (1) the Three Response Systems; (2) the High Road/Low Road; and (3) the HPA Axis and Hormone Release. When we take time to understand the basic science of how the body responds to trauma, it has enormous potential to transform and inform our theology of healing and how we can best respond to victims of violence.

The Three Response Systems

Paul McLean is the neuroscientist who first came up with the notion of the Triune Brain.[2] He divided the human brain into three different categories.

1. *The human (or neomammallian) brain.* This involves complex cognition. Sometimes this is called the "learning" brain.
2. *The mammalian brain.* This is responsible for the fight/flight/freeze response, and it is often considered the adaptive brain.
3. *The reptilian brain.* This involves energy conservation. Sometimes this is referred to as the "lizard" brain.

Although current neuroscience has debunked McLean's theory, his framework does reveal three important brain systems used

---

2   For more basic information on the Triune Brain as it relates to Stephen Porges's work that developed McLean's early work, see Peter A. Levine, *In an Unspoken Voice: How the Body Releases Trauma and Restores Goodness* (Berkeley, CA: North Atlantic, 2010), 97–103. Page 99 shows the phylogenetic hierarchy of response strategies that mimics the original thought of McLean.

in the survival response. If we can put aside his terminology, the image of the brain he espoused can be useful.

During the 2017 Treating Trauma Master Series put on by the National Institute for the Clinical Application of Behavioral Medicine (NICABM), designed to train the leading researchers and practitioners in trauma, it was declared that most professionals agree that this basic framework of system responses is too crucial to simply throw out. They, like me, believe it still offers a helpful way to think about the brain in trauma.[3] In order to account for what is debunked and what we still deem useful, I have renamed these brain systems to emphasize what is important. They are

- the cognitive response (or thinking response);
- the emotional response (or the fight/flight/freeze response); and
- the primitive response (or the tonic immobility response).

Here is a closer look at what these three survival categories look like as it relates to trauma.[4]

Important Brain Regions for the Three Survival Categories

In the cognitive response, the most important brain regions are:

1. The cerebral cortex/neocortex (the outer layer), which includes the four lobes: the frontal lobe, the parietal lobe,

---

3   The Treating Trauma Master Series from the National Institute for the Clinical Application of Behavioral Medicine (NICAMB) with Ruth M. Buczynski, PhD. This program ran for five weeks in October and November 2017.

4   I acknowledge David Lisak's influence through a personal training titled "Applying Science to Increase the Efficacy of the Criminal Justice Response in Non-Stranger Sexual Assault Cases" that took place on October 6, 2015, at Emporia State University.

the occipital lobe, and the temporal lobe. The neocortex is responsible for:

- receiving and processing sensory information
- making sense of the world
- working memory

More specifically, the prefrontal cortex is the foremost part of the cortex, including the frontal lobe. This is where we are distinctly human and where complex cognition takes place.

2. In the emotional response, the most important brain regions are in the limbic system, which is incredibly vast. I want to highlight two main parts:

   a. The amygdala, which searches for danger and threat (outside conscious awareness), and
   b. The hippocampus, which is involved in encoding long-term memory.

   When the limbic system is aroused, the person either fights, runs, or gets ready to fight and run (we call that "freeze").

3. In the primitive response, the important brain areas include:

   a. The brain stem, which contains nerve cells that control heartbeat, breathing, and the glands and muscles used for eating and communicating.
   b. The cerebellum, which is important for body memory and procedural action.

Functions of the Important Brain Regions

As it relates to the trauma response, each of the important brain areas has a specific function to keep us alive. In the cognitive response, the functions necessary for survival include things such as:

- Planning, organizing, analyzing, thinking about best choices
- Problem solving
- Declarative memory: things we can declare that we know

In the emotional response, the important functions we need for survival during threat include various things such as:

- Emotional responses
- Long-term memories
- Fight/flight/freeze

In the primitive response, the functions necessary to survive threat are things such as:

- Conserving energy
- Slowing heart rate
- Slowing breathing

The main goal of the brain stem is to maintain homeostasis (balance) in the human system, and the brain stem is where the implicit (or procedural) memories are stored, which aid us in routine, automatic tasks such as tying our shoes.

Actions of These Brain Regions under Threat

When threat is perceived, the cognitive response includes:

- Being able to think clearly—before immediate and deadly threat is present
- Problem solving

We survive because we analyze and make the best decision possible after assessing the threat. When they cannot think or problem solve, the victim is pushed into the fight/flight/freeze response (the emotional response).

When a threat is so terrible that cognitive thinking is shut down (see the section "HPA Axis and Hormone Release" below for how this happens), the emotional response may include:

- Flight
- Fight
- Freeze (this is more of a freeze to jump into action where the muscles contract, ready to attack or run)

We survive in the emotional response because of the emotional fear reaction caused by receiving information from our five senses. This is an *unconscious* (out of our awareness) survival tactic. It is our body trying to survive. We perceive threat, and the body responds accordingly.

When this fails, when it hits a certain threshold, our bodies respond in the primitive response. *When we cannot answer the question, What can I do to survive?, we move over to the primitive response.* When we can still use our agency to act in effective ways, we are responding from either cognition or the limbic system. When all attempts at exerting choice and control over the situation fail, the primitive response takes over as the body attempts to survive. In the primitive response, we experience tonic immobility. This is when we cannot move. We freeze entirely. Our heart rate slows, our breathing slows, and we become immobile. This is an *unconscious* (out of our awareness) survival tactic. This primitive response is our body trying to survive. Note there is a distinct difference between freezing to prepare for action (this is usually a short-term freeze) and tonic immobility, where the body literally slows down.

The further one moves through the response systems, the more primitive and unconscious the response becomes. This is an important component in understanding the trauma response. Survival responses are not conscious, not thought out, and not planned. In fact, these responses do not access higher cognition. However, this is how bodies are supposed to work in order to stay alive.

For example, perhaps we see a stimulus, what appears to be a furry animal crossing the road (a movement in the corner of our eye). The cognitive response is to say, "Look! A cute little animal," and move on. This is cognition. We see it, and we let it go. You saw, you analyzed, and there was no threat.

However, in less than a second, if the retina perceives that it is not an itty-bitty nonthreatening animal, and if the movement does not continue to give the message that the stimulus is harmless but instead is huge and massive, our biological response changes. A message is sent directly to the brain (and we are not aware of it). When our perception of that stimulus hits a certain threshold, we respond by either running away from that massive stimulus or resisting and fighting it.

The fight/flight/freeze response says: *"Oh, no,* it's a bear!" Thus, rather than thinking—your body decides for you: I'd better run. I'd better fight. Or I'd better get ready to run and fight.[5] But again, this is not exclusively cognitive. Once a threat is identified, the cortex and frontal lobes are not involved in this process. They often shut down with the influx of hormones (see "HPA Axis and Hormone Release" section below).

If we reach a higher threshold of emotion, where we can no longer respond with fight, flight, or freeze, then we move over

---

5   Note that according to Joseph LeDoux in his book *Anxious: Using the Brain to Understand and Treat Fear and Anxiety* (New York: Viking, 2015), the term "fight/flight/freeze" was coined by Walter Cannon. LeDoux also postulates that tonic immobility is different from the freeze response. He claims freeze occurs when "muscles are contracted and poised to be used in fight or flight" (55), and tonic immobility occurs when "the body is flaccid" (55). This is currently a much-debated topic in the study of the neurobiology of trauma, and many are divided on the issue.

to the very primitive response. When we can no longer answer the question, "What can I do next in order to survive?" we have passed the threshold of fight/flight/freeze and have moved over to energy conservation for survival. In this primitive response, which is completely outside of thinking, the body takes over as if to say, "There is nothing I can do, and in a last attempt, I will try to survive by lying here." This is what we call "tonic immobility." Heart rate slows, breathing becomes minimal, and the person cannot move. This reaction is based in the brain stem, and its primary purpose is homeostasis through slowed breathing, lowered heart rate, and basic body functioning.

Brain Response Systems

- Cognitive Response: "Awww, it's a cute little animal."
- Emotional Response: "It's *huge*!!! Run! Fight!"
- Primitive Response: "There's nothing left I can do. I can't fight, and I can't run."

For each brain system, there is a certain threshold (or tipping point) that sends a person into a more primitive reaction to stay alive. Crossing these thresholds is not cognitive or an active choice. The body automatically does these things in order to survive.

If we looked at this threshold changing in images, it would look something like this:

At the cognitive threshold, we can plan, think, and decide the best course of action. At the emotional threshold, the body answers the question, "What can I do now?" But, it is difficult to think and plan. At the primitive threshold, there is nothing left to do. I can only lie here in a last-ditch effort to survive.

The High Road and the Low Road

The second way I teach about the brain in trauma, we call "the high road and the low road."[6] I highly recommend reading Daniel Siegel's research to understand this concept in greater detail. As humans, we sense a stimulus (a sight, a sound, or an experience through the senses), and the information goes to the cortex via the brain stem and other structures in that area. The cortex is the part of the brain that organizes memory and is responsible for problem solving, decision making, and planning. The cortex informs the amygdala (the threat alarm in the limbic system) about what level of threat to perceive about the stimulus. The amygdala functions as the control panel, letting our bodies know if the stimulus is dangerous or not. This cortex-to-amygdala process describes the "high road." The high road carries the stimulus to the sensory thalamus to the cortex to the amygdala. We act and behave after thinking carefully and processing information.

Comparatively speaking, this is an incredibly slow process. The high road takes a lot of time. If we always used the high road, every single stimulus that came into our field of experience would be thought about, analyzed, and processed. It would take entirely too long, and we could not accomplish much of anything. Therefore, we learn quickly with what we call the "low road." It is incredibly fast and gets the information to our amygdala rapidly, without active cognitive thought. This is a good thing. It saves us time and energy.

As toddlers, we learn that we should not run out in traffic, and the low road saves our lives. Instead of standing there and processing each stimulus that gives us the message "car," we instantly are aware—don't run in traffic! This low-road process is a very good thing. Except, of course, when the low road trains

---

6   For one of the best explanations of "the high road and low road," see Dan Siegel, MD, "Interpersonal Neurobiology," YouTube, www.youtube.com/watch?v=aa_3JjkxSsM.

our brains to fear a completely normal stimulus that happened to be present at the time of a threat. In trauma, the low road can be disabling and troubling for survivors.

In trauma, a stimulus that is completely normal and non-threatening (like the smell of freshly baked cookies or the sight of a red door) is bound with the message "danger" in the same way the stimulus for "car" gave us the message "Don't run in traffic!" as children. Our brains are trained in the trauma experience to find similar threats in order to survive later. The low road bypasses the cortex (the thinking, analyzing portion of our brain) and goes straight to the amygdala without any cognition, processing, or problem solving. One can imagine why this would be problematic as it relates to trauma. If a person is threatened and simultaneously they happen to smell baking, it is entirely possible that the smell of freshly baked cookies could be ruined. If a person is assaulted and sees a red door, it is likely that every time they see a red door, their threat alarm system is activated.

Why would this be? The low road serves as a quick way for the brain to respond instantly to a specific threat based on surrounding incoming data. Just as the toddler learns "car," and "Don't run out in traffic!," the next time a survivor smells fresh cookies, their body gets the message: "Fight, flight, or freeze to survive." This is not something the person thinks about or analyzes. It is an automatic low-road survival response. The behavior for survival happens outside of cognition and rational thought. We call this "coupling." The two pieces of information have been coupled together to ensure survival. In this example, the threat and the baking cookies smell are joined together in order to quickly relay a message to the brain.

This means that if our survivor smells fresh cookies again, even if there is no weapon in their face or no real threat present, the brain still perceives it as a threat and responds accordingly. The brain is protecting the body by gathering similar data from a prior threatening experience in order to enable it to survive. This is important to knowing why a survivor is behaving a certain way and understanding what needs to be healed.

HPA Axis and Hormone Release

The final way to explain the brain in trauma is through understanding the HPA Axis and Hormone Release.[7] HPA stands for "hypothalamus, pituitary gland, and adrenal gland." The amygdala detects threat and activates the HPA axis, which results in a secretion of hormones. These hormones strongly influence the resulting behavioral response. The amygdala signals the hypothalamus, which signals the pituitary gland, which signals the adrenal glands.

Adrenal Gland and Hormone Release

The adrenal gland produces many hormones during threat, including catecholamines, cortisol, opioids, and oxytocin. These are the most important ones for this particular discussion. These hormones can be present in the body for four to five days.[8] This is incredibly important for how we respond to a particular behavior following a traumatic event *or* for behavior that follows a repeat coupled stimulus. This hormone release happens in the original

---

7   In the interest of making this work easier for theologians to understand, I have limited the discussion on neurobiology. However, there is also important work done on the polyvagal system (with ways to put on the vagal brake). For more information on this, I highly recommend Stephen W. Porges's work *The Polyvagal Theory: Neurophysiological Foundations of Emotions, Attachment, Communication, Self-Regulation* (New York: Norton, 2011). If the original source proves difficult, I recommend Sharon Stanley's discussion of Porges's work in "Structures and Functions of the Brain and Polyvagal Theory of Autonomic Functioning," chapter 2 of *Relational and Body-Centered Practices for Healing Trauma*. Polyvagal theory is an excellent way to describe the uncoupling of the undesired behavioral response.

8   According to presentations by Rebecca Campbell such as this one: https://www.youtube.com/playlist?list=PLpIlUxHJ-xbp9I6BWri-pRaAgkaORLSZy.

trauma, *and* it often happens when the stimulus is repeated later, even when no threat is present. Our bodies survive and function in life by low-road messaging, but when the low road involves a normal, nonthreatening stimulus, hormones can still be released. Under threat, these hormones are doing really important things to prepare the body for action when there is a threat present.

Catecholamine. This is the adrenaline rush you feel that prepares you for fight/flight/freeze.

Cortisol. Generally this hormone pulls energy available in the body to carry out action. This is the hormone that gets us moving and mobilizes us.

Opioids. These are intended to push away the sense of pain.

Oxytocin. This pushes up good feelings. It is the bonding/loving (nursing) hormone.

The first two of these hormones together enable you to fight or run. But sometimes the energy bottoms out—and you freeze. However, these hormones, although meant to promote survival, also cause us to do things that are a bit more complex. While catecholamine, or adrenaline, is meant to prepare the body for action in threat, when there is too much of this hormone, cognitive thinking is slowed. Adrenaline can act like a big stop sign in the neocortex, blocking consistent access to analyzing, planning, or problem solving. Equipped with the knowledge of what happens when too much adrenaline is present in the system, one can understand why a victim might do and say things that seem less than rational. Their behavior will appear especially irrational to those who do not have an influx of adrenaline in their system and who have consistent access to higher cognitive functioning. Again, this seemingly less-than-rational behavior could last four to five days following the traumatic event itself *or* the repeated stimulus of threat. The body is using adrenaline to prepare for survival action, and this hormone can easily shut down or slow access to that higher level of cognitive thinking.

If there is too much cortisol in the body, sometimes a person can bottom out on energy. Even if the hormone is intended to help gather the energy in our body to carry out fight and flight, it is possible that a flooding of this hormone could drop energy. Thus, it makes sense when we see a victim sleeping for days or appearing depressed. Although opioids are meant to push away pain, too much of this hormone in the body can cause a person to feel nothing. Thus, it makes sense when a victim shows no reaction whatsoever to a traumatic event. We might be tempted to respond with, "Well, they aren't acting like anything happened, so it must not be true." But if that is really the way their body is responding, such a response on our part would be unethical. Although oxytocin is meant to help us bond, as in the experience of a nursing mother and her child, too much of this hormone in the body could cause a person to laugh and giggle after a traumatic experience. Thus, it makes sense that a victim would defend the person who violated them. They have experienced the bonding sensation—because their body produced more of that particular hormone in the traumatic experience.

The point is this: many of the behaviors we judge as problematic are actually biologically based and are how our bodies are designed to respond to threat. It is what keeps us alive. When we judge a person's biology, we become part of the problem and cause secondary harm (if not secondary trauma).

When I speak at community events or train professionals, after an explanation of the body and brain like this, I take the audience back to the three-part Trauma Lens with which we began this chapter. I ask the listeners to consider how many of the answers to the second question (where I ask about behaviors that stem from emotions in trauma) are explained entirely with a better understanding of the body and brain in trauma. Without fail at this point, I watch people's awareness appear on their faces, and I inevitably hear, in almost a whisper, "all of them."

When we understand the biology of trauma, everything from hypersexuality, to a lack of boundaries, to verbal aggression, to self-medicating, to self-harm, to having no response begins to make sense in terms of basic body functioning for survival. We have a body that works to enable us to live in the face of extreme threat. This is a good thing. Therefore, the point of this explanation of the body in trauma is twofold. First, I intend to normalize victim response so we can truly understand what is happening; and second, I hope to provide readers with the knowledge required to create adequate healing methods and access better responses to victims, that consider these basic biological factors.

If we want to help and facilitate healing (instead of causing harm, as so many survivors are telling us), we must take this information into account. Healing from the trauma will be connected to how the trauma happened in the body in the first place. Victim behavior must be normalized. The biological response is not the problem; violence is the problem. When we work toward healing, our methods must take this biology into account. So often, when we speak of healing we are trying to talk about it in terms of cognition (which requires our frontal lobes) to make sense of experiences that are not cognitively based. But here, in the trauma healing experience, we are talking about things our bodies did automatically, outside of our conscious awareness. So, there are two issues:

One, we need to think about trauma outside of only recommending talk therapy. Cognitive-based therapies are great in many respects; but when it comes to complex trauma, we are learning that more is needed. We need tools and a skill set that access the more primitive brain areas.

Two, we need to understand how memory is coded differently when the low road goes straight to the amygdala. We need to find ways to access trauma memories that are outside of active cognition. Chapter 3 will address how we will take these two crucial components into consideration while facilitating healing experiences.

Reference Guide: Signs to Watch for in Survivors That Explain Behavior

SIGNS A PERSON IS HAVING A FLASHBACK[9]

Eyes are looking at nothing.

They are unable to think or problem solve.

You sense they are not there with you but are in the past.

They exhibit shortness of breath.

They are jumpy and startle easily.

They lose gaps of time where they can't remember, or they describe memories as being "all black or blank."

SIGNS OF HYPERAWARENESS OR HYPERAROUSAL (WHERE THE AMYGDALA IS HYPERACTIVE)

They are watching the exits.

Eyes are wide and dilated.

They report sleep or diet changes.

Breathing changes.

They are hypervigilant.

They exhibit destructive behaviors and actions.

They do not see, do not taste, and do not smell.

SIGNS OF HYPOAROUSAL (LACKING ACTIVITY)

They show no emotion.

They have blunt or no affect.

They are not present in the moment.

They have a very low arousal response.

They exhibit a no startle response.

---

9   Note: All of these behaviors are completely normal and expected following a traumatic experience (or chronic traumatic experiences).

Case Study: Teens and Healthy Relationships, LGBTQ

You are the senior pastor who entrusts a roomful of youth (all under eighteen) to a church leader, with the assignment to talk about healthy bodies and healthy relationships. The leader begins with a fun activity intended to get the students up and moving around; when it is completed, everyone settles down to hear more. When the leader starts talking about notions of consent, sexual assault, and control over your body, a young girl starts crying, right there in front of everyone. The leader knows for a fact that this girl came out to her family as a lesbian recently and assumes there is no way she was raped. That's just not possible. Girls don't rape girls, the leader assumes.

The leader continues with the lesson, but the young girl's sniffles and sobs become distracting. So, the leader stands up and asks the group to pause a moment, and the leader takes her out to the hallway. When the young lady calms down, she tells the leader she's been raped. The leader assumes it must be have been a male who forced himself on her and asks who he was. She looks mortified and runs down the hallway into your office. She is hysterical, and the leader is running after her, angry that she's such a problem.

How do you deal with the young, hysterical girl who experienced rape (by another girl) and secondary trauma by a well-intentioned but misinformed church leader?

How do you deal with your church leader?

How can you prevent something like this from happening in the future?

What is the most important thing to focus on in this situation? Why?

3

Healing Imagined

Introduction

It was a warm April evening when I gathered together a group of survivors of sexual assault for an art healing workshop. April is Sexual Assault Awareness Month, so most of the nation's service providers have activities and events going on throughout the month. On this night, I partnered with a local rape crisis center and led a workshop from "A Window Between Worlds," an art-based trauma healing method,[1] for an evening of fun and healing.

Through the last few years of research and observing, I noticed many assault survivors have no desire to attend an event where they will be forced to talk about and think through their worst memories of violation and violence. However, if I bring art to the occasion and focus on empowerment, more people are willing to give it a try. Art and other activities tend to shift the pressure off of the moment because opportunities to be creative help the survivor want to participate. Before long, participants are lost in the experience and are actually having fun.

---

1 See AWBW.org. According to the website, "art is a catalyst to opening windows of safety, self-expression, and connection" (accessed May 29, 2018).

For this workshop, I intentionally set aside space to think about safe places. We advertised this as an evening to consider what safety means for each one of us by creating an art project. As the event began, I asked each participant to give me one word, just one simple word, to tell me how they felt at this moment. In the "A Window Between Worlds" curriculum, we call that a "one-word check-in." The point of this activity is to entice my participants to buy in to what we are doing. I want them to give me one word, in the beginning, in the hope it is the start of getting them to speak about their own narrative as the workshop progresses.

However, I also make it very clear that there is no pressure ever to talk or participate in any of the activities offered. This is also a crucial component of what "A Window Between Worlds" teaches. Sometimes survivors will participate by passing every opportunity to speak, and this is perfectly acceptable. Others will participate by answering every question and doing everything I propose, and this is also OK. Sometimes participants will use the art supplies in the way they want instead of how I instruct, and this is also perfectly fine. The healing art workshop is the survivors' space. I just offer suggestions. Everyone is free to do what they feel is most comfortable.

So we begin with one word to start the event. I usually answer first. I feel "excited" or "hopeful." I often hear survivors talk about feeling anxious or timid because when we start and actually sit down, often the idea of art combined with their most horrific experience can make them a bit nervous. But this is good. I watch their raw honesty. They tell me this is a little different, and I celebrate that. I look into their eyes as they tell me their word, and I validate it. My goal is to communicate: *Yes, I see what you feel. What you feel is perfectly acceptable, and thank you for having the strength to tell us.*

For this April workshop, as the evening progressed, I carefully guided the group through a series of activities. First, I had them all imagine and picture in their mind's eye what their safe space looked like, felt like, even smelled like. I had them pull into their subconscious and figure out who or what was in their safe space. Next, I asked them to draw and color, and to actually create their safe space. I had them pull from their minds (often just outside of awareness) and create it on paper in front of them. This is where it gets really fun. Participants forget what they are there for and they start getting into the experience. They play and laugh, even start chatting among themselves. This is how I know things are progressing well.

When they finish their art, I ask them to tell the group about it. In my experience, this is one of the most crucial pieces of the healing process. The survivor can create amazing art in these moments; but when they put words to it, assigning language to communicate to their friends why they created what they did, a whole new level of healing is possible. As they speak their narrative out loud to the group, a whole other level of awareness comes to light.

However, I must also stress, the response of the group is also important. If the group members (and especially me, as the leader) do not really hear and feel what the survivor shares, healing is often stunted. During any confessions or words that a survivor shares, I stay present, make eye contact, and really hear what they say. I also validate what they feel and continue to thank them for finding the courage to tell us. This is a truly important piece.

By the end of this event, my group of survivors felt lighter and seemed to find more meaning in their chaos. I could look at each of their faces and see something shifted for them. This whole process of the art healing workshop is specifically set up in a way that sets apart space (or a "container," as I will show later in this chapter) and provides a platform for the survivor to be heard and felt in their agony and their strength. Each participant was also free to have fun; to get lost in the moment, and experience time where they did not have to think. Almost ironically, it was in the moments they did not have to think that a cognitive awareness fertilized and then was able to come to life in the words and images they shared.

In chapter 2 I showed how easy it is to cause harm to the brain's ability to cognitively process information. Violence intimidates another human in a way that creates a biological reaction that continues to affect access to cognition and active thinking, even when the threat has passed. This threat survival activation does not simply fade away. In order to keep the body safe and alive later, the body and brain work in a way that searches for similarities to the threat. This means normal situations might seem threatening to a survivor of violence. It also means their bodies often react in paradoxical ways for quite some time. Unfortunately, as seemingly simple as it is to cause harm to response systems, healing these same spaces takes incredible work and effort. Healing is not a quick and easy fix—and it certainly was not completed in one night in April—but it is possible. Healing is a journey, a process into learning how to live with a new biology and thrive anyway.

In this chapter you will find a framework for how communities of faith can work toward being helpful for survivors in their healing process and not harmful. However, I must also stress that religious professionals need to know their limits. Although not everyone is gifted to offer healing tools, all members of the faith community can find ways to let their words reflect the types of healing I offer (see chapter 5 for more details).

In other words, although I use this chapter to show reasons why certain healing methods tend to work and describe how healing might be set up to be the most effective, this does not necessarily mean every church leader, every pastor, or every professional is equipped to do this process. With that disclaimer, though, I do say that every church community and professional can borrow from this instruction and learn how to select their words and responses better when interacting with survivors of violence.

The point I want to keep making is this: it is easier to open healing paths for survivors of violence and assault when all people involved truly understand what we are helping to heal, when we understand what biology we are dealing with, and if we approach survivors without judgments of their behaviors during trauma or following a trigger of trauma. As faith leaders, we might not be the ones actually leading the healing journey; a trained professional will be doing that. However, we are an important part of this healing process. The more we understand about the various components and select words and responses that coincide with what professionals are doing, the better will be the result for survivors.

This chapter introduces healing and provides an overview of the work done by Thema Bryant-Davis, showing how healing after trauma is about thriving rather than an ending of all symptoms. This chapter will also incorporate Sharon Stanley's work on synaptogenesis and myelination as the neurobiological explanations for how healing happens after trauma.

I offer four foundational recommendations:

1. Use ceremony to release pain and facilitate healing.
2. Tell stories to enable the survivor to feel seen, heard, and felt.
3. Create opportunities that do not require active problem solving or analyzing.
4. Employ methods of consolidation or integration.

I also offer four recommendations for how these four foundational concepts can work:

1. Body movement
2. Artistic creations
3. Writing
4. Mindfulness

Healing

Healing is what is hoped for after the experience of violence. There might be damage to the body, harm to skin, bones, mind, and the spirit, but people generally want to believe there is a potential for healing. Thus, we must decide what constitutes healing.

Thema Bryant-Davis claims healing does not end with "the cessation of all symptoms" but instead results in thriving.[2] I appreciate this definition because it allows healing after violence to be understood as much more complex then healing after catching a germ-based sickness. Bryant-Davis defines thriving as "empowerment of the survivor to regain his or her voice, body, power, and sense of self."[3] In other words, thriving is about gaining power and control over your voice and body after such power is taken away in the experience of violence. It is about recognizing that power and living into it.[4] For a common illness or sickness, healing would mean there are no more symptoms. When we have the flu or cold, healing is ending of things like coughing or sneezing.

Healing from violence is about thriving and living well, even though there was trauma caused by a violation of autonomy.

Several key researchers and practitioners inform our understanding of how we create healing modalities. I will discuss two of them here: Sharon Stanley and Pat Ogden.

---

2 Thema Bryant-Davis, *Thriving in the Wake of Trauma* (Lanham, MD: Altamira, 2005), 6.

3 Bryant-Davis, 6.

4 Christy Sim, "Body, Theology, and Intimate Partner Violence: Healing Fragmentation through Spiritual Play" (Diss., St. Paul's School of Theology, 2014).

Sharon Stanley's work has transformed healing research. She claims there are two primary ways the brain can change after violence.

1. **Synaptogenesis** "for connections between intact neurons and those that have been damaged."
2. **Myelination**, referring to the "fatty myelin sheath that coats the axons on the nerves of the ventral vagal social engagement system that moves information and energy very quickly through neural networks" so that "fear is transformed with connection."[5]

According to Stanley, one way we heal is by uncoupling the connections that are no longer appropriate for survival (for example: connection #1, *threat,* and connection #2, *fresh cookies,* as in the example in chapter 2).

Humans begin healing when there is a separation of the threat from the nonthreatening object. In this instance, freshly baked cookies are disconnected from death potential, and now cookies become a nonthreatening object again. Cookies are just cookies. The other way we begin to heal, according to Stanley, is through human connection that changes biology and how the brain functions. Safe, good, relational connections can impact healing.

Both of the healing methods Stanley describes interrupt the unneeded survival processes of a traumatized brain. Both synaptogenesis and myelination help to bring cognition forward to understand what the primitive brain is already doing to respond to a prior threat. We will look at each of these methods in more detail.

---

5 Sharon Stanley, *Relational and Body-Centered Practices for Healing Trauma* (New York: Routledge, 2016), 52.

Synaptogenesis

Synaptogenesis uncouples the inappropriate connections between a completely normal stimulus and the threat response. It is about uncoupling the vagal nerve response (the motor or sensory response) and pulling it out of the autonomic system's fear response (or survival reaction). Synaptogenesis is about uncoupling the unwanted and unneeded behavior with the feeling of perceived threat. It is about changing how the person's threat response system relates to the environment following a traumatic experience.

Synaptogenesis helps to uncouple the negative behavior or reaction from the stimulus by:

- Uncoupling the automatic reaction to stimulus
- Uncoupling the survival tactic response to the stimulus

We know healing is happening through various signs as:

1. Feeling the body as it is, sensing where the body is in space. Or coming home to the body, as Sharon Stanley terms it.[6]
2. Tactics to ground in the present moment (rather than the past threat or fear for future threat).
3. Bilateral stimulation (which often brings a person into the present)—something like walking or squeezing a ball between two hands.
4. Combining a sensation and new message (example: touch a stone and think "I'm valuable") and working to make this the strongest neural pathway.
5. Reactivating choice options.
6. Connect neurons not previously connected, so that learning takes place.

---

6 Stanley, 61.

7. Making meaning of the biological reaction, utilizing cognition.
8. Awareness of what's inside and outside the self (or conscious and unconscious).
9. Feeling emotions as they are.
10. Being present in the energy of the moment.

Myelination

Myelination is about transforming fear through connection. This is about empathy, someone truly feeling the intensity with a person who experienced trauma. Myelination is also about establishing eye contact, even with animals. Healing through myelination is something all of us can take an active part in as we relate to survivors of violence. We can help survivors feel seen and heard in all the intensity of their trauma experience. We can also work to help survivors feel trust toward us in our relationship, and we can find ways to offer affirmation. All of these help the process of myelination.

We know healing is happening through signs such as

1. making connections with other humans;
2. expressing emotions in a safe space;
3. feeling like we are in a safe space;
4. having fun with others;
5. feeling a sense of belonging;
6. touch (when desired); and
7. connecting with animals.

These two means of healing consider the body's reaction to trauma, survival tactics, automatic bodily reactions, and the basic neurobiology of trauma as described in chapter 2. These healing methods are *not* about how we might go back to the way things were but instead thrive, despite what violence did to the body and brain. This is a key component to understanding healing after violence. Healing is about moving forward in the present and thriving even though the brain was rewired from trauma.

Others propose we think of healing in other ways. For example, in the October and November 2017 Trauma Master Series put on by NICABM, Pat Ogden proposed there were two ways we can help people heal after the experience of violence:

1. Vertical Integration

   - This notion of healing integrates three pieces of the brain: the thoughts and belief systems
   - with emotional integration (when rage or terror is felt)
   - with primitive integration (where it manifests in the body).

In other words, we begin to heal when we can integrate all the parts of the trauma experience in how our brain responded in the moment of threat.

2. Other Integration

   - This notion of healing integrates the right brain and the left brain
   - when the body is ready for fight/flight/freeze (and the amygdala is dominant) with
   - an awareness of the body's experience. In this case, the traumatized person becomes more aware when their body does something. Or, in other words, the person is cognitively aware of what they previously did subconsciously.

All of these ways to explain how we heal, whether Stanley or Ogden, help us to imagine healing from the starting point of the body. In other words, we begin to heal when we can integrate all the parts of the trauma experience in how our brain responded in the moment of threat.

Four Foundational Recommendations

I offer four foundational recommendations for imagining the healing of the body's normal and expected biological response to the threat of violence and the experience of trauma. All of these recommendations build on Stanley, Ogden, and others.

1. Use Ceremony to Release Pain and Facilitate Healing.

Sharon Stanley's work describes the use of ceremony. Stanley regards ceremony as a "container" to hold the "chaotic, undifferentiated energies of trauma and allow transformation."[7] In the development of healing tools, ceremony is an important piece. It is the place we set aside and protect for a specified moment in the healing experience.

Ceremony is a set-apart space that organizes behavior in a compartment of time for remembering, releasing, and processing.

Creating the space for healing is an important first step in setting up the healing process for victims of domestic violence and sexual assault. This includes intentionally creating the space for the ceremony. This "ceremony" becomes the container for healing.[8]

---

7   Stanley, 75.
8   Stanley, 75. Sharon Stanley says several important things for this point: "Healing practices can be amplified through ceremony, a set of actions that create a crucible for the dynamics of change. Ceremonies can hold the intense, chaotic, undifferentiated energies of trauma and allow transformation to occur a natural, communal way, restoring interconnectedness and inviting the fragmented elements of the right hemisphere to come back into cohesion" (75). Later she says, "A ceremony involves encounters that contain and hold disturbed energy of trauma

According to Stanley, ceremonies should

1. clarify the intention to care for the self and the other;
2. offer an embodied greeting to start. This is a "mindful" greeting "involving a respectful presence and welcome, a moment of eye gaze, naming of the other, and physical guidance with gesture and movement into the space";[9]
3. give new material to metabolize the relationships;
4. provide silence for synthesis through body based awareness in time, space, energy, and connection to the environment; and, finally,
5. result in a coreflection (on the shared experience).[10]

Stanley instructs that healing is ceremonial and must take place in healthy empathetic relationships. When an organization creates these ceremonies through their healing tools, healthy empathetic relationships must also be factored into the objective of creating ceremonies. Based on this and my experience of survivors in ceremony,[11] I offer a fivefold activity specifically designed for victims of domestic violence and sexual assault and based in

---

along with the natural healing forces of life" (77). Stanley continues, "The ceremony can be a contained intersubjective dialogue between two people or a group; it might be a meditation, or the experience of sharing and embodying imagination and dreams, dancing, music, or other expressive forms" (77). Finally, she says, "The elements that make it a ceremony include embodied intersubjective relationships, the rituals of sacred, uninterrupted time, the development of bodily-based rhythm and movement, and somatic relational exploration of internal and environmental influences on human experience" (77).

9 Stanley, 78.
10 Stanley, 78–79.
11 Use of texts on ritual include Anne R. Bewley, "Re-Membering Spirituality: Use of Sacred Ritual in Psychotherapy," in *Women's Spirituality, Women's Lives*, eds. Judith Ochshorn and Ellen Cole (New York: Haworth, 1995), 201–13; and Anthony J. Blasi, *Ritual as a Form of the Religious Mentality* 46 (1985): 59–71.

Stanley's research. I use these in any healing activity I lead with survivors (and even with professionals when dealing with vicarious or secondary trauma).

These ceremonies act as containers to create space for healing and should include:

1. Focusing the intention and putting words to why we are gathered together
2. Providing new material in order to accomplish the goal
3. A body-based action step (something to do with the body—whether it is an exercise or anything else like tearing paper or moving around)
4. Co-reflection and integration in order to make meaning of the shared experience and
5. Gratitude and closing

If we desire to set up spaces for the healing work, the use of ceremonies as a container for the procedure can be a helpful component because it sets aside space and intention for a moment on the healing journey.

2. Tell Stories to Enable the Survivor to Feel Seen, Heard, and Felt

I encourage anyone who wants to speak and respond in ways that are healing for people who experience violence to ensure there is a safe space for the survivor to tell their story, in the right place, at the right time, so that they feel seen and feel heard. We must be intentional about bearing witness to the stories of a violation of autonomy. To bear witness to the story does not mean we have to be present for the violence but instead means we must be present to hold the story of violence.

When I lead a support group, art healing workshop, or any other healing method for survivors, the purpose of multiple participants gathering together is for them to be witnesses for each other.[12] The other members and the leader should provide a living witness to trauma and resilience in the contained space of the ceremony.

Flora A. Keshgegian, in her book *Redeeming Memories: A Theology of Healing and Transformation*, outlines three very important components for healing through remembering. These are: recalling the suffering, remembering the strength, and incorporating both into a new narrative. I will discuss each of these in more detail.

1. *Recalling the suffering.* Keshgegian claims that the way we recall the suffering of victims is through "preservation and by honoring all who died and all that was lost."[13] This means we must truly feel and experience the suffering of another in empathetic connection. Why is this step so important? Keshgegian says it is because these things are too easily erased and forgotten.[14] If true healing will take place for victims of violence and assault, we must fully recall and hear the pain of the trauma experience in all its intensity. We hold the memory of the extreme trauma for the survivor.

---

12 In *Relational and Body-Centered Practices for Healing Trauma,* Sharon Stanley adds several important pieces to this discussion: Stanley says there is a "power of the community to heal trauma" (81). She also says, "A strong community where people are welcomed *as they are* and are connected through their heritage, through day-to-day living and shared arts and culture offers a sense of home for people suffering from early trauma and a solid container for the restoration of wholeness for an individual" (83). Later she adds, "Somatic empathy communicates to people suffering from trauma that they are seen, felt, and understood just as they are, allowing them to *feel felt*" (4).

13 Flora A. Keshgegian, *Redeeming Memories: Theology of Healing and Transformation* (Nashville: Abingdon, 2000), 28.

14 Keshgegian, 28. "It is important to recall and remember the suffering and losses that are threatened by forgetfulness or eraser."

2. *Recalling the strength and resilience.* However, Keshgegian does not simply leave us in the pain and agony. She recommends that we also find the places of resistance and resilience. In every instance of trauma, there are moments of amazing courage, strength, and resilience. We just need to find them, hear them, and highlight them back for the survivor. Keshgegian claims this is what bears "witness to the resilience and persistence of the human spirit."[15] As we are looking for these moments of strength within the narrative of a survivor of violence, we even notice what the survivor did in the moment to survive the threat. Keshgegian says that this is about recognizing "what she did to enable her survival, including the use of defense mechanisms such as dissociation and denial."[16] Thus, in this step, even the body's unconscious (and sometimes embarrassing) reactions are celebrated. Survivors are incredibly strong. We just need to find the moments we see this strength and show them what we observe.

3. *Incorporating both recollections into a new narrative.* Once the story of trauma has been truly heard and felt in all its intensity—both negative and positive, the survivor can begin to incorporate the full experience into a new narrative. In other words, Keshgegian says, "It is vital to remember life experiences beyond or alongside those of victimization and resistance, and to incorporate them into a more encompassing narrative."[17]

The first narrative after the experience of violence is confusing, often creates feelings of shame, and is filled with self-doubt. But the second narrative that emerges after the first two steps

---

15 Keshgegian, 29.
16 Keshgegian, 54.
17 Keshgegian, 29.

is about "developing a different narrative of life; it entails a type of reconstitution of self, including self in relation with family and society."[18] It is about thriving in the moment, even though a traumatic incident occurred and changed the body and brain.

These crucial pieces of remembering, mourning, celebrating, and reintegrating must be incorporated into healing tools for survivors. If we want to have a voice and role in healing after violence, these pieces are important assets. When we provide victims with carefully constructed safe spaces, whether with us personally or in a group setting, they will be free to tell their personal stories of suffering and resilience, which need to be truly heard and seen, in order to incorporate both into a new narrative. It is important to note at this point that without a story being truly heard and seen in the right spaces at the right time, moving forward is not likely. This is so important that without it, survivors are left feeling lost, confused, and alone (all things that mark retraumatization).

Unfortunately, because we tend not to know why survivors behave the way they do and make the choices they do (based in the neurobiology of trauma), we can make unfortunate judgments. Survivors hear it all and feel something is wrong *with them*. In the face of such unfair judgements, a container is never created and the stories of loss and resilience are never heard and seen. Survivors, rather than feeling that we connected with them in empathy (in all its intensity), feel different and unworthy.

3. Create Opportunities that Do Not Require Active Problem Solving or Analyzing

The third foundational recommendation for those who provide healing tools for domestic violence and sexual assault survivors is an openness to creating opportunities that do not require active problem solving or analyzing.

---

18 Keshgegian, 29.

Consider how we respond to a disclosure of domestic violence or sexual assault. It often becomes apparent that we are ill-equipped to deal with the complexities of violent trauma, and we make a referral to a counselor.[19] Counseling often involves talk therapy, which actively requires access to higher cognition. Although this is a great tool, it is not enough for victims of violent trauma. Talk therapy (alone) does not tap into the more primitive response systems involved in fight/flight/freeze or energy conservation that were active in the trauma experience. We must find ways to access the more primitive and unconscious spaces in our healing methods.

The best counselors and therapists for domestic violence and sexual assault survivors are those who incorporate healing methods that aim to activate the most primitive and unconscious parts of our brain.

What is the unconscious space, and what do I mean by "unconscious" versus "conscious"? According to Cathy Malchiodi, LPCC, "the unconscious is defined as the part of the mind not available to consciousness."[20] In other words, what is not in our cognitive awareness is in our unconscious. For example, most of us do not walk into walls on a regular basis. This is because our subconscious awareness keeps track of where the walls are, even though we are not consciously thinking and analyzing where each wall is located. Our unconscious is important for survival. The

---

19 According to the February 2017 release of "Domestic Violence and the Church Research Report," sponsored by Autumn Miles through Lifeway Research, 76 percent of American Protestant churches have a procedure in place to refer a person experiencing domestic violence to a trained counselor. See Bob Smietana, "Good Intentions, Lack of Plans Mark Church Response to Domestic Violence," LifeWay Research, February 20, 2017, https://lifewayresearch.com/2017/02/20/good-intentions-lack-of-plans-mark-church-response-to-domestic-violence/.

20 Cathy Malchiodi, *The Art Therapy Sourcebook*, 2nd ed. (New York: McGraw-Hill, 1997), 31.

key point of understanding the unconscious parts of the brain is this: traumatic experiences fall back to an unconscious survival modality, and thus healing must also tap into this. If the trauma moments are experienced and recorded in the memory in ways that are not conscious (and we are not completely, consciously aware of them yet) we must find ways to access the brain system that was present in the trauma.

There are several ways to think about how we might access the spaces that are beyond active cognition through problem solving and analyzing. One place where we see this in in contemplation. Christine Valters Paintner has published extraordinary work on contemplation. She claims that with contemplation, "we open ourselves to listen and ponder" and "we move our awareness into our hearts and let our vision arise from this place of integration rather than analysis and receptivity."[21] In other words, contemplation occurs when we set aside analyzing and instead become aware in the heart space (or the emotional space). Contemplation involves an awareness in the "heart" rather than an awareness in the mind. This is important because in this space, outside of cognition, the brain's response systems are active in the trauma experience. This is the primitive response of energy conservation and the emotional response of fight, flight, or freeze. Then in the cortex, where we process information, the brain response systems analyze, think, problem-solve, and are aware.

Contemplation begins in the area of the brain outside of active cognition to first encounter the body's reactions before we cognitively process, think, and declare meaning.

In anatomical terms, contemplation is what happens in the space outside our neocortex (outside our planning, problem solving, and analyzing), in order to have a cognitive awareness of

---

21 Christine Valters Paintner, *Eyes of the Heart: Photography as a Christian Contemplative Practice* (Notre Dame: Sorin, 2013), 30–31.

those things that are noncognitive (such as trauma responses). In this other space, outside of thinking, we encounter the spiritual and begin to know ourselves more deeply. Once we touch this space, our minds become more aware. In other words, almost ironically, it is by setting aside the more active cognition that this same cognition is then enhanced. It is in this non-cortex-knowing space that we actually know ourselves better.

There are many ways one can practice contemplation. These range from practices such as meditation to photography. A person could even participate in "contemplative walking," where one allows oneself "to not have to 'get' anywhere" but instead listens to their "own intuition" about where they "are being moved to go next."[22] There truly are endless options for contemplation and how one might practice it.[23] However, what is important is that regardless of what one selects to activate contemplation, it happens through the choice of releasing control over thinking about what will happen in order to allow spiritual eyes to see through the heart. This practice acts as a springboard into the healing process and thereby allows one to experience thriving.[24]

Meditation is often regarded as a way to activate contemplation and is a concept known to neurobiologists. Neuroscientist Sara Lazar speaks of a need to allow the brain to meditate. Meditation allows the brain to reflect on itself.[25] We are able to know ourselves and actually think more clearly about situations when we give the brain a chance to take time off and perhaps

22 Christine Valters Paintner, *The Artist's Rule: Nurturing Your Creative Soul with Monastic Wisdom* (Notre Dame: Sorin, 2001), 35.
23 See my "Body, Theology, and Intimate Partner Violence," 55.
24 Elsewhere I propose that spiritual play practices are key factors.
25 Brigid Schulte, "Harvard Neuroscientist: Meditation Not Only Reduces Stress, Here's How It Changes Your Brain," *Washington Post*, May 26, 2015, https://www.washingtonpost.com/news/inspired-life/wp/2015/05/26/harvard-neuroscientist-meditation-not-only-reduces-stress-it-literally-changes-your-brain/?utm_term=.9dfd2ba3606c.

even have fun. I recommend that those desiring to have a voice and role in healing should create opportunities for contemplation, and I believe this can happen effectively through play. Here people can rest from thinking in order to heal. This is also the space that is often activated in worship services through the arts (music, art, dance, and beyond).

4. Employ Methods of Consolidation or Integration

It is important that all healing activities begin with an understanding of the brain and body's response to trauma. In other words, healing activities must include an understanding of the experience of trauma, including a person's inability to act, feeling close to death, being overwhelmed, and losing agency. When we truly understand the body and brain's response to violence, we can begin to develop tools and responses to survivors that promote healing. In addition, I encourage all healing modalities to include the three response systems of the brain, as was discussed extensively in chapter 2, in order to facilitate opportunities between active cognition, what we experience emotionally, and what we feel in the body.

What is integration? According to Daniel Siegel in *The Developing Mind,* integration "refers to the way the mind establishes functional flow in the states of mind across time."[26] Integration is crucial for a sense of meaning, "coherence, and continuity."[27] Integration is how our minds understand and apply meaning to various moments in our lives. Thus, the fourth foundational recommendation for healing involves a consolidation or integration of what is happening in the body with an understanding of the past, the desire to survive the future, the ability to organize information, and the way to find meaning.

---

26 Daniel J. Siegel, *The Developing Mind: Toward a Neurobiology of Interpersonal Experience* (New York: Guilford, 1999), 8.

27 Siegel, 9.

To make these four foundations a little simpler and easier to remember, here are four words that began with the letter *C*. In whatever we do for healing after violence, I recommend these four *C*'s:

1. Ceremony with:
    a. Focus of intention (why we are here)
    b. Goal (providing new material to accomplish the goal)
    c. Body-based action (activities that use the body and tend to distract the mind)
    d. Co-reflection and integration (making meaning together as we reflect on the activities)
    e. Gratitude (sending off in a positive closing)
2. Community
    a. To bear witness to the trauma and resilience
    b. To provide spaces for trauma survivors to feel seen, heard, and felt
    c. To provide opportunities for persons to validate each other and normalize their experiences
3. Contemplation
    a. Intentionally setting aside active cognition in order to encounter the spiritual or divine (in order to know yourself more clearly)
    b. First, an awareness of the heart, and then an awareness of the cognitive space
4. Consolidation
    a. An integration of the body's response, emotions, and a cognitive understanding
    b. A way to begin to apply meaning to a situation that is incomprehensible

These four foundational concepts can be integrated into our small group studies, Sunday school classes, retreats, worship services, and much more. When they are used, I highly recommend partnering with a community resource or finding someone in your congregation who can help meet the needs in your community.

We know statistically pastors and faith leaders are dealing with survivors on a continual basis, and therefore these recommendations will help you to be more effective in how you communicate with survivors in ways that promote healing and not harm.

Four Recommendations for Healing Activities

These recommendations are based on everything outlined above and recognize that creativity combines the cognitive brain, the emotional brain, and the brain at rest. Whenever I encourage survivors to find what is "playful" for them, where they can stop thinking and just experience, I ask them to name their favorite thing to do. Sometimes it is art. Sometimes it is sports or music or drama. Play is whatever gets them into a notion of "flow"[28] and having fun, where they let go of vigilance, overactive responses, and just relax.

According to Cathy Malchiodi, play is important for even adults: "It is behavior that enables us to feel free to explore and express without self-judgement or inhibition, to participate for the sheer joy of the experience, and to think creatively, flexibly, and innovatively."[29] I agree and find it crucial for the journey toward healing. When we play we let go and just experience the activity in all its fun and glory. Play taps into those moments where we look at the time and wonder what happened and how long we have been participating in an activity. It is fun and freeing. And in the fun, we can find healing.

Healing is about

- social connection and belonging, being heard and experienced;
- integrating the body's experience with cognitive awareness and emotional response;

28 See Mihaly Csikszentmihalyi, *Flow: The Psychology of Optimal Experience* (New York: HarperCollins, 2009) for more about "flow" when time passes quickly and we are in the moment.
29 Malchiodi, *The Art Therapy Sourcebook*, 58.

- playing while the body is relaxed and the brain is thinking and feeling simultaneously in "flow"; and
- finding ways to discover meaning in an incomprehensible experience of trauma and violence.

There are at least four basic ways to play our way to healing:

1. Body movement, exercise
2. Artistic creativity
3. Writing, journaling
4. Mindfulness

Some people do not like exercise but love art. Others hate writing but do not mind jogging for a mile. I find that almost always, a survivor can fit into one of these four categories to play their way to healing.

Let's look at each of these four play activities in a little more depth.

1. Body Movement

Often, the body in motion helps the brain cognitively process information. Experts encourage any exercise that enables "cortical alertness."[30] When our bodies are moving and active, our frontal lobes are able to process information and cognition can get online. Examples of body movement: walking, running, jogging, yoga, dance, breathing exercises, water activities, jumping rope, boating, hiking, biking, and flying a kite.

2. Artistic Creativity

Artistic creation can take many forms; most engage the senses, and all involve components of nonverbal expression.

a. Art (tends to be dominant in the sense of sight)

---

30 Pierce J. Howard, *The Owner's Manual for the Brain: Everyday Applications from Mind-Brain Research* (Austin, TX: Bard, 2006), 223.

b. Music (tends to be dominant in the sense of sound)

c. Culinary (tends to be dominant in the sense of taste and smell)

All of these artistic experiences involve certain components of rhythm, sequence, balance, and control over selected tools. For example, art tends to have a rhythm of spacing, a sequence of order, balance of colors, and control over the outcome. Music uses rhythm but also involves a balance of notes, a sequence of harmony, and control over the instrument or voice. Each artistic activity has basic components that utilize the senses and are expressed nonverbally. I recommend art as the primary tool initially after trauma. This is because, at first, trauma is unspeakable, literally wordless.

According to Cathy Malchiodi, author of *The Art Therapy Sourcebook*, "Researchers have discovered that traumatic experiences often become encoded in the mind in the form of images. That is, when we experience traumatic events" our minds encode memories similar to the way a camera takes a photograph.[31] Thus, Malchiodi argues, "visual art may offer a unique way to express traumatic images, bringing them to consciousness in a less threatening way."[32] This is my experience as well. Whenever I lead an art healing workshop through A Window Between Worlds,[33] I start with art. It is a lot less threatening to draw out what makes us feel safe than it is to show up to a counseling appointment and talk about the worst experience of our lives. It is much easier to draw squiggle lines that describe how we feel than it is to find words to talk about what we are feeling. Words are difficult to find after trauma.

---

31 Malchiodi, *The Art Therapy Sourcebook*, 10.

32 Malchiodi, 10.

33 See a sample workshop, "Touchstones: A Creative Journey," AWBW, http://awbw.org/art-community/touchstones-a-creative-journey/.

As I lead art workshops, I try to access a few words along the way. I help participants through a process where I help them finding meaning. First, we begin with our *hands expressing art*; second, I ask them to begin to *write* about what they artistically created; and, finally, I request they *tell the group* about what they created. Using the preverbal combined with written, and then adding the verbal, helps survivors find their voice as they apply meaning and comprehension to their experience of trauma. In other words, I recommend we use nonverbal art to springboard us into some cognitive thinking and finding words. Here are examples of artistic creativity: manipulating clay, making poems from a book page, cutting out meaningful magazine photos, assigning colors to feelings, painting, using coloring books, cutting paper into a design, shattering dishes to make new art, writing a song, baking a cake, smashing cookies for a dessert, making mashed potatoes, drama, drumming a rhythm of how they're feeling, or creating coin/leaf rubbings.

3. Writing and Journaling

Writing is a practice that draws you inward to discover things about yourself that you may not have in your cognitive awareness. When you write, self-knowledge comes out of your body and sits on the paper or screen. Instead of having this knowledge stuck in the mind, writers create words that can be reread until one's knowledge or experience makes sense or feels less threatening. Writing brings self-knowledge out of concept and into actuality, much like art, but with language.

Writing is also a practice that can often make us feel as if we are beginning to gain control of the narrative of what happened to us instead of feeling as if the narrative is controlling us. When we write things out, we can see them all lined up and organized. We can let go of holding onto the memory because it is written down and accessible if we need it again. This is very similar to the experience of letting other community members hold the story with us. At the core, writing holds the memory for us. Writing puts our story and experience into words not only so we can see it and be aware but also so others can bear witness to it. Artistic creativity has elements of this, but it is in words that we find language for our experience.

James Pennebaker offers incredible research in the area of writing. "Actively holding back or inhibiting our thoughts and feelings can be hard work," he writes. "Over time, the work of inhibition gradually undermines the body's defenses. Like other stressors, inhibition can affect immune function, the action of the heart and vascular systems, and even the biochemical workings of the brain and nervous system."[34] In other words, Pennebaker tells us that when we try to stop our thoughts and feelings or keep them in the theoretical, it can harm our body. We need ways to release our thoughts and feelings for the sake of our health.

Writing is one of the ways we can stop that inhibition and let out our thoughts and feelings. As Gillie Bolton says, whereas *talking* is something that disappears "on the breath" and *thinking* is "harder to remember reliably," *writing* creates a record of "interests, concerns, wants, and needs."[35] Writing holds the moment in a tangible way.

So why should one bother with the energy it takes to write?

   a. *It is good for your health.* In several of James W. Pennebaker's studies, he found that those who wrote about "their deepest thoughts and feelings surrounding trauma evidenced an impressive drop in illness visits."[36] In fact, in one study, compared to a control group (where they were instructed to write about superficial topics), those who

---

34 James W. Pennebaker, *Opening Up: The Healing Power of Expressing Emotions* (New York: Gilford, 1997 revisions), 2.
35 Gillie Bolton, *Write Yourself: Creative Writing and Personal Development* (London: Jessica Kingsley, 2011), 11–13.
36 Pennebaker, *Opening Up*, 34.

wrote expressively about their deepest thoughts and feelings about their trauma saw a 50 percent drop in illness visits to the doctor.[37]

b. *It builds immunity.* In a second research project, Pennebaker and his team took participants' blood samples to study, in addition to their writing assignments. They found that "people who wrote about their deepest thoughts and feelings surrounding traumatic experiences evidenced heightened immune function compared with those who wrote about superficial topics."[38]

c. *It builds confidence.* In a third study, Pennebaker and his research team studied men who had been laid off in their careers. They found that "within 3 months, 27%" of those who wrote expressively "landed jobs compared with less than 5% of the men" who had done "no writing." By a few more months, "53% of those who wrote about their thoughts and feelings had jobs, compared with only 18% of the men in the other conditions."[39]

d. *It reduces anxiety.* In a 2015 study based on Pennebaker's work, scholars at an Italian university replicated his research by assessing participants' levels of anxiety both before the writing sessions and four months after the sessions. They found that expressive writing helped with reducing anxiety *up to four months* after the initial writing research.[40]

Writing is a way to

- stop the inhibition (of holding back thoughts and feelings); and

---

37 Pennebaker, 34.

38 Pennebaker, 37.

39 Pennebaker, 39.

40 Joshua Smyth, "Effects of Writing about Traumatic Experience," *Journal of Social and Clinical Psychology* 34, no. 6 (2015): 495–507.

- put words to an event and put words to the emotions of an event.

Writing helps a survivor make sense of chaos and begin to integrate the experience into one's life. Examples of writing activities: "finish-this-sentence exercises," writing a page about one's self, writing a mantra, making positive statements about one's self, describing talents and abilities, starting a list of other people's compliments about one's self, writing how and where a person can feel safe.

4. Mindfulness

Mindfulness is the practice of being fully present in the moment. According to Pat Ogden and Janina Fisher in their combined project *Sensorimotor Psychotherapy: Interventions for Trauma and Attachment*, there are five building blocks of being in the present moment:

a. *Cognition.* This concerns such things as "thoughts, interpretations, meanings, beliefs about ourselves, others, and the world."[41]
b. *Emotion.* Emotions involve "subtle nuances of feeling tones and mood (e.g., a sense of peace or slight irritation)."[42]
c. *Five-sense perception.* This is the "internally generated sense perception" of "smell, taste, sight, touch, and hearing (e.g., scents, flavors, images, textures, sounds)."[43]
d. *Movement.* This includes "gross motor movements (e.g., postural changes, gestures, facial expressions) and micro movements (e.g., trembling, the pounding of the heart)."[44]

---

41 Pat Ogden and Janina Fisher, *Sensorimotor Psychotherapy: Interventions for Trauma and Attachment* (New York: Norton, 2015), 138–40.
42 Ogden and Fisher, 138–40.
43 Ogden and Fisher, 138–40.
44 Ogden and Fisher, 138–40.

e. *Body sensation.* This is about "the physical feelings (e.g., tingling, vibrating, shivery, dull) created as the various systems of the body monitor and give feedback of inner states."[45]

These five building blocks of the present moment help us understand how to focus our intentions in order to be mindful. As you read this book, you can practice understanding this exact moment by focusing on what you are thinking, feeling, sensing in your perceptions, moving, and body sensations.

When we are fully present in the moment for mindfulness, we find ourselves connecting with our innermost vulnerabilities. In this space, we do several things:

- Validate our own strengths
- Stop the internal dialogue and just be
- Learn to be comfortable with silence
- Find a willingness to be honest with our own questions, concerns, and doubts
- Connect with our own narrative
- Find compassion for ourselves, even in errors
- Bump into our own biases
- Become safe in our own head

Note: I do not recommend this healing modality for those barely out of trauma, because the silence and inner dialogue can be too overwhelming. I recommend starting with helping the brain feel safe long before it recognizes the present moment. The point of these recommendations is that each of these play practices helps us encounter the vulnerable moments in ways that are less threatening as we name the experience in images, words, or actions. Then we are able to release the energy caught up in not understanding and the confusion we feel after the experience of trauma.

---

45 Ogden and Fisher, 138–40.

Case Study: Her Behavior Seems Like the Problem

Jenna is a teenager who has a tendency to be slightly dramatic and comes from a difficult family life. She treats every difficulty in her life like a huge mountain to climb, asking for attention from everyone in the church. Suddenly Jenna will start withdrawing from speaking or talking much at church events. After a few experiences of this, you ask Jenna what is going on with her. She breaks down and confesses she was raped by another teen in the youth group.

At this point you do everything right. You help her file a report, teach her about the forensic exam, and help her consider her options. You also refer her to a local service provider who can meet her counseling needs. However, several months later, Jenna's behavior seems to be outrageous. She's caught lying and stealing. Everything is more than dramatic; it is a life-altering shake for everyone in the community. Jenna is also now telling everyone about the rape, so now everyone is aware. She seems to want to talk about it constantly.

As the pastor or leader, you feel in over your head. You want to help, but the patterns of behavior are incredibly disturbing. You want to be there for Jenna, but you also don't want to enable or create more drama. What can you do?

Remember to consider:

1. The brain responds to normal stimuli differently after trauma.
2. Behaviors after trauma tend to be paradoxical.
3. What would it be like to be trapped with someone who you have to see all the time in your faith community?
4. The behaviors of victims are often indications of something much deeper. Focus on what is deeper, not necessarily the behavior.

Pastor/Expert Q & A

Pastor Joe: For my sermon Sunday, what would be the best and most succinct way to say that you're never obligated to put up with abuse?[46]

Expert: I think that is a pretty good start. Be direct. You are never obligated to put up with abuse, ever. I would say something along the lines of: "If you're being harmed, you never deserve to be hurt. Nothing you could ever do would be enough to cause you to deserve to be harmed." When you do this, it is a round-about way of saying that when your abuser says it is your fault, it is not. To receive this message at church would be incredibly powerful for a victim.

I had a survivor tell me once, "He hit me, but I deserved it" (and whatever it was she did that made her think she deserved it). So I got drastic in my response. I said, "I don't care if you insulted his manhood, made fun of his mother, or accidently baked glass in your casserole, you still don't deserve it." It got the point across that there is nothing this woman could have done to deserve to be harmed. (Sidebar: it can be abusive to insult manhood and make fun of someone's mother, I know, but my point was to pick the worst possible things to make sure she understood that as a pregnant woman, there was absolutely no reason for her to be thrown around, ever).

Pastor Joe: What do I say in my sermon that addresses the person who knows abuse is not their fault but feels like it might be their obligation to stay?

Expert: Again, be direct. You've already got it: "It's not your fault, and there is no reason you have to stay. Not biblically, not spiritually, or any other reason." I think then I would say something like: "If you are being harmed, there are great resources

---

46 These questions and answers are based on typical conversations I've had with pastors.

in our town to help you. If you decide you want to get out of a harmful, abusive relationship, know that your safety and your wellness is most important. God doesn't want you to be harmed. God wants you to thrive and be safe." Then have those resources available. Know your community service providers. Have pamphlets and cards and whatever else your town has. Be prepared.

I would suggest putting something on the insides of the bathroom stall doors about how people can access help if they need it. That simple act does more than give out information. It also sends a message to the congregation that abuse is not acceptable in our community. I also recommend putting statistics, resources, and quotes in the bulletin for months that focus on awareness about violence. Here is a summary:

January: Human Trafficking Awareness Month; National Stalking Awareness Month
February: Teen Dating Violence Month
March: "No More" Campaign (one week)
April: Sexual Assault Awareness Month; Crime Victims' Rights Week (one week)
October: Domestic Violence Awareness Month

The important thing is to keep your survivors in mind when you preach and speak. The fact that you want to communicate from the pulpit that violence is not acceptable or the victim's fault is truly amazing. If all pastors even thought of asking this question, the whole world might shift.

———

Pastor Chantel: How do we give the message to forgive others but not communicate that if one partner abuses the other, the one abused should just forgive and take it? How do we balance the tension between these two?

Expert: I think this must begin with a solid understanding of forgiveness. What is forgiveness?

- Is it acceptance of the offender?
- Is it holding the offender accountable?
- Is it trusting the offender?
- Is it letting go of anger?
- Is it releasing the hold the act of violence has over you?
- Is it restoration?
- Is it restored relationship?
- Is it a releasing of guilt for wrongful actions?
- Is it allowing the story to be told in its entirety and truly heard?

Once we *know* what we are saying about forgiveness, that shifts how we balance the tension. For example, if we say forgiveness is about letting go of anger, we also say, "and some anger is holy anger. I think even God is angry about how you were violated." If we say forgiveness is about accepting the person again, then we add a disclaimer that in cases of violence, we understand this may never be possible.

The point is, we cannot shove victims into letting go of anger and forgiving simply because it is in the doctrine. We do more damage when we push people into forgiveness before their bodies and brains even processed the trauma and offense. Sometimes the strongest thing a survivor can do is refuse to forgive because they have not reached that point in their healing journey. For a survivor of violence, not forgiving can be an act of agency, standing up for themselves and doing what is best for them.

It is not a popular opinion, but I am convinced that in some cases of violence, forgiveness (true forgiveness, where each person is on an equal plane with equal power) will never be possible in the survivor's lifetime. A victim can only do so much and go so far without the participation of the offending party admitting responsibility for the extensiveness of their damage, without seeing any justice, and without being equal in power to the person who violated them. I believe forgiveness is a relational concept for an entire community that involves:

1. Both parties admitting the extensiveness of the damage. This means the victim has to actually understand what happened to them and be far enough into the healing process that they can apply meaning. This can take years. This also means the offender needs to do serious work in understanding the results of their actions and truly understand the part they played in the trauma.

2. The offender admitting the extensiveness of the damage without being honored for it (in other words, no standing ovations).

3. The victim being truly heard and feeling felt while being lifted up and honored by the community.

4. The entire community honestly admitting the extensiveness of the damage to the victim (and whatever part they played).

5. The victim receiving adequate and efficient justice from the church community, the social community, and anyone else involved.

6. Both parties being on an equal field where both have the same power. One is not a victim and one an offender—they are equal.

7. Both parties having control over their agency and being active participants in the process. No one is forced to forgive or asked to forgive before they are ready.

Sometimes the strongest and most amazing thing a survivor of violence can do is accept the fact that they can only go so far in the forgiveness process. Anything a survivor does, or doesn't do, in regard to forgiveness is something that takes incredible strength. I don't think we honor and respect this enough.

Pastor Chantel: How does it honor Jesus to tell a victim to turn the other cheek?

Expert: It does not. In fact, it does not honor anyone. I do not believe that passage was meant to keep the oppressed in oppression.

Pastor Chantel: How do we speak of forgiveness and reconciliation without giving abusers more tools for shaming and blaming?

Expert: Always think about what you are saying and preaching through the eyes of a victim. How would a woman (who is beaten at home or terrorized verbally) hear what you are saying? How would a man (who is not allowed to leave his room, except for church) experience what you are saying?

In seminary we are trained to imagine the perspectives of those in our congregations, and this is no different. A pastor or leader might not know exactly what people are dealing with at the time when it comes to family violence, but always attempt to hear your message through the ears of someone being violated and oppressed at home by an intimate partner (or family member), because statistics prove that it is happening.

––––––––

Rev. Shannon: As a pastor, when an abuse situation arises in your church, which party do you support?

Expert: Desmond Tutu said, "If you are neutral in situations of injustice, you have chosen the side of the oppressor." The same is true here. Domestic violence is a horrible experience of someone controlling you and taking away your agency. It is a terrible injustice. We cannot be neutral about violence. If we are neutral, several things happen:

- We send the message to victims that they are without support.
- We fail to hold offenders accountable for their actions.

The most loving thing you can do for a perpetrator of violence is hold them accountable. This is how you support them.

Rev. Shannon: How do we know who is the victim and who is the perpetrator?

Expert: When I look at the entirety of the situation, I can usually tell what is going on in the domestic violence situation. The tools I use to determine who is being victimized and who is perpetrating are not just something I have as an expert. You can discern these things too.

1. Who seems to hold the power over what is said?
   - The one with this kind of power is probably not the victim.
2. Who feels that they are not allowed to say certain things? Or suddenly starts spilling a lot out because they feel free to let things loose for the first time?
   - This person is most likely your victim.
3. Who doubts what they do constantly?
   - Again, this is most likely the victim.
4. Who blames themselves (when they shouldn't)?
   - A perpetrator rarely takes the blame but finds ways to shift it off of themselves and onto anyone else.
5. Who takes responsibility for their actions?
   - A perpetrator rarely owns up to all their actions.
6. Who is quick to prove why it's another's responsibility?
   - A perpetrator is brilliant in ways to reassign responsibility on everyone but themselves.

One time I saw a text message of a male telling a woman that she was such an abuser and that she lied and he had proof. And immediately, I knew he was the perpetrator. A victim would most likely never do several things that are communicated in that text:

- Call their abuser names;
- Make extravagant accusations; or
- Use "you" when making claims (like "You are such a liar").

Why would a victim not do this? Because it is incredibly dangerous! But an abuser would and twist it to make it seem like the victim is the abuser. The woman's response to the text further indicated to me that she was the victim. She overthought every single word she typed back, and it all started with the word "I." So things like, "I am sorry you feel that way" and "I simply need to know when to pick up the kids" (and so forth). She made no accusations, engaged in no name calling, and put everything in the first person. Her overanalyzing to make sure she did not upset him further was quite telling. If you pay attention, the words said between two people are very indicative of who is the abuser and who is the victim.

If I really cannot figure out who holds the power and control because they are both doing the things I'm looking for, I usually ask a question that helps me figure it out. So, for example, I will say: "If you told her not to go to work tomorrow, would she do it?" Then I flip it around: "If she told you not to go to work tomorrow, would you do it?" The answers to these questions are very telling because the one who is not allowed to go to work when demands are made is probably the victim.

Know that you will not always get it right. I am an expert and I still make mistakes. Sometimes an abuser is so good—so crafty and so knowledgeable—about victim behavior that they can fool even me. It's rare, but when it happens and I discover I was wrong, I apologize and take responsibility for my actions. If you mess up, apologize and do the same. We are not 100 percent accurate. We do our best and try to be loving, but sometimes we make mistakes. It is how we act after our error that makes the difference.

4

Vicarious Trauma

Introduction

My son was flying into our local airport one day, and I was so excited that I probably caused concern among the TSA employees with my joyous bouncing. When his plane arrived and he walked out, I hugged him tightly; I was so thrilled to have him home. I had him in one of those "don't ever leave your mother again" grips when he made a noise and said, "Mommmmm, you're choking me."

Even at that moment, when I was so happy to see my child, I had to stop myself from responding: "Oh, please. Choking is internal; strangulation is external." I did not say it out loud, but my brain immediately went to all the information I carry both in expert knowledge from training and what I hear survivors say about their personal experience of being strangled.

In this joyous moment when I should have been focusing on the present happiness, my brain went to another place. As I kept hugging my son (a little lighter, of course), I also had to step back mentally because I realized I had vicarious trauma.

I have never experienced strangulation; however, I was responding as if I had. My breathing sped up, my heart started racing, and I started shaking as I thought about all the horrific details of what we know about strangulation. As I processed this over the next few weeks, I remembered reading Laura van Dernoot Lipsky's book *Trauma Stewardship* a few years prior, where the author talks about having visited a gorgeous mountain scene. She was with her family and should have been focused on the moment, experiencing the beauty around her. "We had hiked to the top of some cliffs on a small island," she writes, "and for a moment, the entire family stood quietly together, marveling, looking out at the sea. It was an exquisite sight."[1] She describes "turquoise water as far as you could see, a vast, cloudless sky, and air that felt incredible to breathe."[2]

However, as she stood in the middle of one of the most amazing views, her thoughts shifted. She asked herself, "I wonder how many people have killed themselves by jumping off these cliffs?"[3] That is when she realized that her work with trauma had really began to affect her. "I had always considered myself a self-aware person," she wrote, "but this was the first time I truly comprehended the degree to which my work had transformed the way that I engaged with the world."[4] Just as I did in the airport that day with my son, she realized she had symptoms of vicarious trauma.

Most of us who encounter trauma regularly find ourselves having a similar experience at one point or another. We all have a happy moment influenced by the trauma of others, and it changes how we perceive the world.

This chapter focuses inward to help you think about how to care for yourself before, during, and after giving pastoral care to those suffering from domestic violence and sexual assault. We

---

1 Laura van Dernoot Lipsky, *Trauma Stewardship: An Everyday Guide to Caring for Self While Caring for Others*, with Connie Burk (San Francisco: Berrett-Koehler, 2009), 1.

2 Van Dernoot Lipsky, 1.

3 Van Dernoot Lipsky, 1.

4 Van Dernoot Lipsky, 1.

will address self-care, understanding signs and symptoms, and much more.

Vicarious Trauma

Laura van Dernoot Lipsky says a vicarious trauma response occurs "when external trauma becomes internal reality";[5] in other words, when the external experience of someone else is internalized within us and it affects how we see and interact with the world.

VICARIOUS TRAUMA (also called secondary trauma or compassion fatigue) is when you get so wrapped up in the traumatic experience of another that you exhibit physiological, psychological, and spiritual responses as if you were the one who experienced the primary trauma. Vicarious trauma shifts how you perceive and engage with the world.

Vicarious trauma happens when we care about another person. This is something most of us tend to agree is a good thing: caring about other people. We care, we feel their pain, we empathize; and before we know it, we can easily take on their trauma as our own. It can happen to anyone. There are no superhuman leaders who are exempt from experiencing secondary trauma. No matter how experienced you are, no matter how many agonizing tragedies you have walked through with people, and no matter how convinced you are that your heart is made of steel, you can still find yourself with symptoms of vicarious trauma—simply because you care.

As Laura van Dernoot Lipsky so vulnerably shares, "I was certain that this work [in trauma] was my calling, my life's mission. I was arrogant and self-righteous. I was convinced that I was just

---

5   Van Dernoot Lipsky, 42.

fine."[6] But just like her, at some point many caregivers experience secondary trauma and are forced to deal with the fact that we are just like everyone else, susceptible to not being fine. However, in spite of the fact that this happens frequently, it does not mean we are all doomed if we care about people. There are tools we can use to recognize when it happens and to mitigate the effects of secondary trauma.

If I left myself in the moment of pondering strangulation instead of taking steps to take care of myself, I could have spiraled out of control. However, I was prepared for this moment. I knew it could happen to me, no matter how smart I was or how much I knew. I was ready to use tools to mitigate my experience of vicarious trauma. The same was true for Laura van Dernoot Lipsky, and her courage to face her own secondary trauma changed how all of us view and respond. I trust that you, too, will find the strength to face the fact that you may experience trauma vicariously.

Before Vicarious Trauma

1. *Be aware of signs and symptoms.* One of the first steps in preparing for vicarious trauma is to recognize and be aware of when you are experiencing signs and symptoms. You can google "signs of vicarious trauma" and come up with a plethora of examples. These are a few of the signs and symptoms I have commonly seen happen with advocates who work with domestic violence and sexual assault:

- Not caring about the same things that you once cared about
- Acting like another person's crisis is your crisis
- Losing sleep or sleeping too much
- Not eating or too much eating
- Withdrawing from people

6   Van Dernoot Lipsky, 2.

- Seeing the negative when you should be enjoying the present positive
- Feeling put off by people in crisis
- Not being able to find words or language for what you feel
- Experiencing an exaggerated startle response because your amygdala thinks it needs to protect itself from a danger you never experienced personally
- Feeling stuck, as if you will never move past this feeling, emotion, or space

If you can prepare yourself to recognize the symptoms, it empowers you to be ready to act before you find yourself in the moment. Just like victims, when we experience secondary trauma, our brains do not work in the usual way. When we feel the effects of vicarious trauma, it is a lot more difficult to access our cognitive functioning, to process the current moments. However, if we think about how we will respond ahead of time, we can be prepared and know what to do when we are needed.

David Lisak, expert in repeat perpetrator behavior in sexual predators, tells this story from the American Civil War. He said when soldiers went back to the fields of war, after the fighting, they discovered that soldiers had been trained to shoot weapons but not how to load and shoot. So they found several guns that never had been loaded and fired properly. Lisak's point was that before these soldiers went into battle, they received training that became procedural memory (memory that is accessible in extreme threat and to which the cerebellum, which does not use cognition, reacts). However, their training fell short. They were taught only how to reload over and over, not reload and then shoot. Therefore, the training (and thus the procedural memory) was not sufficient for high-trauma situations.[7]

---

7 Notes from my class with Dr. David Lisak on April 2, 2015.

One goal of this book is to help you think through these important issues now and practice them in your body to make them a procedural memory. This chapter will teach you how to work with your active cognition now to be ready for the moments it slips away. Through the activities in this chapter, you will be prepared for the potential of experiencing vicarious trauma and being able to mitigate the negative and harmful effects.

2. *Be aware of yourself.* Have you learned about the famous ancient Greek saying, *"gnothi seauton"* (know thyself)? This is one of the most important tools for mitigating the negative effects of secondary trauma. If we know ourselves, we can recognize when we need to take care of ourselves. But this is also where we confront our biases. Do we think poor people are lazy? Do we consider the homeless a problem? Is dealing with victims an annoying part of our day? What are our biases? We must know them and confront them so we do not cause damage.

Answer these questions:

- How do you pick your friends?
- Why do you pick them?
- How long can you focus on one word or topic before you shift to something else? Seconds? Minutes?
- What can you focus on without interruption?
- What do you feel inside your gut when you hear the word *victim*?
- How have you been known to respond to someone who discloses violence?

3. *Identify your triggers.* People who say they do not have triggers are only fooling themselves. Our brains are designed to respond automatically to various stimuli. This is how we function easily and move throughout daily life. Triggers are things that automatically cause an action, as the brain perceives something similar to a prior experience. Not all triggers are bad. Some triggers are quite useful and helpful for survival. For example, smelling

a certain perfume might trigger memories of your mother. It is also helpful not to have to analyze every stimulus, such as one that lets you know there is a wall in front of you. We take mental shortcuts all the time.

The problem with triggers, however, occurs when the stimuli reminds the brain of a prior experience where life was threatened, and it sends the body into survival actions that are not helpful to the situation. For example, if a person was eating chips when he watched a car smash into the front door, it is possible that every time thereafter when he smelled chips, his brain took him back to that trauma and he reexperienced feelings of terror. Chips are not necessarily bad in themselves, but when coupled with terror, they become a trigger that stimulates a survival reaction in the body.

Maybe not all of us have felt the closeness of physical death, but I have yet to meet an adult who had no experience with the threat of losing someone or something they loved. If we are unable to face our own experiences of social trauma or physical death-imprint trauma, we will not be as helpful to others in crisis.

Activity: Identify your triggers.
What events in my life have been traumatic?
What has been my experience of physical trauma?
How do I typically react to perceived threats?

Activity: Analyze behavior and thinking in response to trauma.
In what ways was I overwhelmed in my capacity to
    respond?
How did this experience change the way I view the
    world?
When am I reminded of these moments? Where am I?
    What am I doing? Who am I with?
How do I respond when I remember? What do I think?
    What do I do?

4. *Know your biases. Know what you think and feel when you encounter various experiences.* It is because we have triggers to normal stimuli that we also have automatic feelings and thoughts when we experience those triggers. This activity will help you think through some of the common biases.

Activity: Finish each of these sentences.

When someone discloses to me that they experienced violence,
    I think (cognitive) . . .
    I feel (emotional) . . .
    I feel (in body) . . .

When I hear someone is accused of sexual assault,
    I think (cognitive) . . .
    I feel (emotional) . . .
    I feel (in body) . . .

When I see someone suffering,
    I think (cognitive) . . .
    I feel (emotional) . . .
    I feel (in body) . . .

When I see a parent sick or in grief,
    I think (cognitive) . . .
    I feel (emotional) . . .
    I feel (in body) . . .

When I see a child harmed,
    I think (cognitive) . . .
    I feel (emotional) . . .
    I feel (in body) . . .

When I hear a scream of pain,
    I think (cognitive) . . .
    I feel (emotional) . . .
    I feel (in body) . . .

5. *Find release techniques.* Find physical ways to let go of the anxiety, fear, and negativity in your body. Peter Levine's work shows how the body needs to shake off the experience of trauma. In his book *The Unspoken Voice*, Levine tells the story of how he was in an accident and immediately tried to allow his body to do exactly what it needed to do. In the ambulance, he was shaking, releasing the built-up energy from his fight-or-flight response.[8] Levine's body perceived the threat in the accident, and he wanted to survive. He wanted to run or fight back, but he could not. The accident itself prevented him from employing mechanisms for survival to run away or fight back. Instead of fighting back or running, he could not respond. That energy to fight or flee is like a spring, bound in the body, until we can figure out how to let go of it. So, Levine, being the expert in releasing this spring, let his body shake in the ambulance until the energy to fight or flee found its completion. "By listening to the 'unspoken voice' of my body and allowing it to do what it needed to do," he says, "I came through mercifully unscathed, both physically and emotionally."[9] Not surprisingly, allowing his body to release energy helped him significantly later.

Our bodies, even as counselors, pastors, academics, leaders, and advocates, also need to experience this shaking off of built-up energy. It can happen when you are forced to slam on the brakes in your car or in response to any other common daily event. Our bodies are created to respond to threat with fight or flight, and when we do not get this opportunity (whether it is stopped by a car accident pinning our body or a human violating us), that energy has nowhere to go. It just stays pent up in the body, like a spring.

I learned a method at the National Sexual Assault Conference years ago called Trauma Release Exercises (TRE) that specifically

---

8   Peter A. Levine, *In an Unspoken Voice: How the Body Releases Trauma and Restores Goodness* (Berkeley: North Atlantic, 2010), 9.

9   Levine, 9.

attempt to trigger the muscles that are supposed to help with fight or flight. These exercises intentionally target the psoas muscles that flex and move to support your core, your internal organs. This method teases those muscles, ever so slightly, and allows the tremor (or shaking) to gently release itself. It is truly one of the most amazing things I have ever experienced. There are many other methods as well; for example, a commonly used technique designed to release the emotional response of the amygdala is EFT (Emotional Freedom Techniques), often called "tapping." At first it seems weird, but it is intended to literally tap on the body's meridian energy points that speak to the central nervous system. Another method is EMDR (Eye Movement Desensitization and Reprocessing), in which the goal is to stimulate the brain bilaterally in order to process overwhelming and threatening stimuli.

Whenever I lead a group through something that requires thinking deeply or about something difficult, I always have them stand (if they can) and squeeze their right shoulder with their left hand, then shake it out. Then I have them squeeze their left shoulder with their right hand, then shake it out. Then I ask them to shake out their legs, move their torso, and so forth. I do this because I am helping provide a way to physically release some of the tension they may have from talking and thinking about tough topics. It is important to intentionally create ways to release the spring of energy in our bodies.

There are many ways we can release this tension and shake it out. Get creative. The point is to release the bound energy that comes from everyday experiences (like slamming your brakes at a stoplight) or more extreme physical trauma (like an accident). If you can release that built-up energy for fight or flight, your body is healthier and able to deal with a current crisis better. There is also fascinating research on how being unable to release the spring might lead to serious illness.[10]

6. *Their crisis is not your crisis.* It is so important to realize and believe that the crisis of another person, no matter how close they are to you, is not your crisis. Sometimes, when I am in the middle of walking with someone through trauma, I have to take a deep breath, orient myself to the location, touch something and feel a texture, and remember that I am in this present moment with them in *their* crisis. I am not in my own crisis from the past, and I am not experiencing a threat of death in body or socially in this moment. It is another person's crisis that I am experiencing. I remind myself that I am self-differentiated.[11] Sometimes people's responses to their own crisis moments are so intense that the words "their crisis is not your crisis" has to become a mental mantra for me, chanted repeatedly, so I can stay present with them in the moment. I know that if I am unable to separate myself from their crisis, I cannot be an active listener in their experience. If I am unable to separate myself from their crisis, I cannot choose words that are helpful and do not cause harm. I know if I am unable to separate myself from their crisis, I cannot truly empathize, get down in the middle of the pain, and feel it with them. If I want to offer genuine pastoral care where I am capable of feeling the pain and grief *with* them but not *for* them, I must be able to know and feel in my body that this experience it is not my crisis, and it is not my threat in this moment.

I want to emphasize that being self-differentiated and maintaining a degree of objectivity is not simply an act of will. It takes practice and having one's own supervisor and/or therapist. Offering empathy is an act of offering compassionate feeling with another person. Empathy is not intrusive; although congregation

---

10 Robert C. Scaer, "The Neurophysiology of Dissociation and Chronic Disease," *Applied Psychophysiology and Biofeedback* 26, no. 1 (2001): 73–91.

11 This is a term borrowed from Bowenain Systems Theory.

members can experience it that way. That is a primary reason that trust and clear pastoral boundaries are so important.[12]

7. *Develop a self-care plan.* Self-care is a popular buzzword. A lot of people assume it means you should take more bubble baths. However, self-care is so much more.

SELF-CARE is the ability to notice and be aware of your own triggers, identify your needs, and proactively develop coping mechanisms to trauma and crisis.

I find that very few people seem to really understand how to make self-care happen in their own lives. It is a lot harder than it sounds. I can remember when my domestic violence therapist told me to practice self-care. I looked at her and timidly said, "And how do I do that?" I will never forget her response because she was not exactly sure either! Neither of us had a starting point to begin to figure out the ways I could take care of myself.

Discovering a self-care plan that would work for me was a long journey from that day in the domestic violence shelter. There was trial and error. I played with one thing and realized it did not help at all. I tried another, and it helped a little. Then one day, after I sat in a sexual assault training, multiple days in a row, hearing the worst and most horrific experiences that can ever happen to a human being, I decided I needed to go hug some puppies. It was a random but powerful idea. I took my husband and daughter, and we loved on some puppies until our faces were wet with kisses and we had laughed so hard that I completely forgot the stress of the day. I realized that when I have to deal with incredibly heavy topics, like violence, I need to spend a little time with baby animals. That is my self-care plan. It is really that simple.

---

12 For more about empathy, refer to the classic work by Heinz Kohut, *How Does Analysis Cure?* (Chicago: University of Chicago Press, 2013).

The following tools are designed to help you discover what would be helpful for you personally.

Developing a Personal Self-Care Plan

- The best self-care plans *are not* planning to do something you don't already do regularly (although it is something you enjoy doing).
- The best self-care plans take into account the things you love to do, the places you love to go, and experiences that bring you great joy.
- The best self-care plans are flexible and ever-evolving.

Activity: Brainstorm and make a list of the following:
Things I love to do.
Places I love to go.

When you are stressed out or overwhelmed, come back to your list. Do the things you love to do, and go to the places you love to go.

Too often we try to make self-care extra work. We try to do what we think we are supposed to do; but a good self-care plan involves actively doing what we already love and enjoy. Whenever I attend a sexual assault training, you can guess I will insist on going to play with puppies. There is something about having a tiny little dog lick your face, climb all over you, and chew your hands that provides the joy I need after hearing horrific things all day. Find what you love and do that.

Developing a Church Community Self-Care Plan

Communities of faith also suffer trauma; for example, the death of a child or key leader, fire or other destruction to the church building, or significant loss of financial support. Just as the best individual self-care plans involve things we personally love to do, churches need to develop their community plan in ways that will be helpful for them.

Brainstorm and make a list of some of those things.

- Regular fun activities in our church community (potlucks, talent shows, special events)
- Fun things our church hopes to do in the next two to three years

Having policies and procedures in place to deal with crisis can also be incredibly helpful. If you have a staff or board, work together to figure out how you can deal with vicarious trauma. It will happen at some point. Make a plan.

After we walk through a crisis, we will

- Step 1.
- Step 2.
- Step 3.

Experiencing Vicarious Trauma

In the moments when I experience vicarious trauma, there are certain tools I carry with me to make it through the experience. When I realize I am trying to claim someone else's trauma as my own, I have to find ways to keep myself in the present moment. I cannot go back to my own prior trauma. I cannot go into their trauma. I must stay grounded in this moment. Know that as someone with significant trauma history, this is hard for me. On the one hand, it makes me the most qualified to walk with someone who is experiencing the same. I really do understand. On the other hand, it requires effort and energy to stay present.

Here are some tools I carry when I become aware that I am experiencing vicarious trauma or I am walking with someone in their trauma.

1. Remind myself to breathe. This sends the message to my brain that I am safe.
2. Touch things around me with various textures. This reminds my body that I am in this space here and now.

3. Glance around my surroundings and identify colors. There is blue. There is red.
4. Randomly do math problems to solve in my head. This works because if I have to subtract 64 from 88 in my head, my cognitive thinking is forced to come online. Because I do not know 88-64 automatically, it takes effort for me to recognize the numbers and figure out how to solve the problem.
5. Walks. I often go for walks in a place where there is beautiful scenery. The bilateral stimulation of walking helps me process various components consciously and subconsciously. My body becomes involved in the process, and I do not have to force it; I just walk and let it happen. Sometimes I need to walk a lot before anything happens. The point is that I am moving and being intentional.
6. Art. Sometimes I draw, color, and do all sorts of artistic creations. Often there are no words for what I feel (whether it is because I cannot explain what I did not experience or it is because the trauma is so overwhelming there is no language to explain it). So I turn to art.

Often folks will tell me they want nothing to do with coloring or drawing. They are not creative, and they certainly are not artists. This is fine, of course, if art is not your thing; no one is going to force it. However, I urge people to at least try it. Your work does not have to be displayed on social media, be hung on your office door, or exist beyond the moment. Art helps you put images, shapes, and scribbles to experiences where language is difficult to assign. I can assure you that the things I see fall out of my artistic pages usually surprise me. Art brings out things I am not yet consciously aware of.

So let's think about this a little more. Why is art such a helpful tool? Art comes from images, right? That seems obvious. But let's go back to understanding trauma. We perceive a stimulus that causes our bodies to respond. That stimulus is often something we see, an image.

The goal in healing art is to process something our lower-brain functioning has experienced that we cannot cognitively deal with (at least yet). So, I let things spill out on the pages, not trying to make them beautiful or usable. As I see the images, it often enables me to find words and use my cognitive thinking to assign language.

These are six of my examples, but do what is best for you. Create a plan now, before you are in the middle of a traumatic situation with someone. If you think about it and plan for it now, you will remember to do it (in that procedural memory), even when your cognition wants to take a break. Be sure to think through what works for you and carry it with you in the moment.

After Vicarious Trauma

Once someone identifies that they have indeed experienced symptoms of vicarious trauma, it is important to step back and breathe. Yes, breathe. When we experience anxiety, we often stop breathing, so there is a lot of wisdom in the common expression, "Take a deep breath." Laura van Dernoot Lipsky describes how she stepped back and made changes in her life to become a person who lives by trauma stewardship. "I knew that if I wanted to bring skill, insight, and energy to my work, my family, my community, and my own life," she writes, "I had to alter my course."[13] She did this through two steps. First, she decided to "take responsibility for acknowledging the effects of trauma exposure within" herself.[14] And second, she "had to learn how to make room" for her "own internal process—to create the space within to heal and discover what I would need to continue."[15] So, (1) acknowledge the fact you experience other people's trauma,

---

13 Van Dernoot Lipsky, *Trauma Stewardship*, 4.
14 Van Dernoot Lipsky, 4.
15 Van Dernoot Lipsky, 4.

and (2) make space in yourself to heal from the experience of others' trauma. I think this is incredibly brave. If every pastor and religious professional could follow these steps, I think this kind of courage could change the faith community forever.

Here are some practical ideas for after vicarious trauma:

1. Keep taking care of yourself.
2. Value your time for you.
3. Know the experience is completely normal and you're a good person for caring enough to experience vicarious trauma.

Power and Privilege: Working with Vulnerable Populations

It would be irresponsible to simply set faith leaders up to take care of themselves, know themselves, and prepare for vicarious trauma without also speaking to issues of power and privilege and what this means when working with vulnerable populations such as victims of domestic violence and sexual assault.

There are various components of our lives we need to check and review in ourselves before we work with a vulnerable population. If someone calls you to walk alongside them, discloses an experience of violence to you, or chooses to come to you for help, you can automatically assume you hold power and privilege. You are the one walking, empathizing with, helping, and guiding; and thus, by the very nature of your position, you are the one with power in the relationship.

As they say, with power comes great responsibility. So, let's talk about what this means. Again, Laura van Dernoot Lipsky is helpful here. "When we talk about trauma in terms of stewardship," she says, "we remember that we are being entrusted with people's stories and their very lives."[16] This is important work and

---

16 Van Dernoot Lipsky, 6.

"an incredible honor."[17] But most significant, she reminds, is that to participate in another's trauma journey requires we remember "the privilege and sacredness of being called to help. It means maintaining our highest ethics, integrity, and responsibility every step of the way."[18] When we walk alongside victims and survivors of violence, we acknowledge the power we hold. As we practice pastoral care among vulnerable populations, we admit the responsibilities that come with having power, and we honor the sacredness of being able to help.

I knew a pastor who was asked to walk alongside a victim of repeated strangulation, gun violence, and one of the most horrific cases of domestic violence I have encountered. He did not see it as a privilege or an honor. He did not view the sacredness of the moment. For him, she was a problem, a burden. Because of how this pastor viewed the situation, he abused his power in ways that caused irrevocable damage to this survivor. He was sure he knew what was best for her and made demands. She followed them, even though they are not what she would have chosen, and she regretted it later. Why did she follow the pastor's demands? Because he held the power in the relationship, yet he failed to see it, acknowledge it, and handle that power responsibly.

If we really want to provide powerful, healing pastoral care to survivors of domestic violence and sexual assault, we must honor the sacredness of the moment, acknowledge our position of power, and maintain our highest ethics and integrity.

Case Study: Not the Preacher?!

Julie is a dynamic woman. Everyone in the congregation at First Church adores her. She sits in the front of the sanctuary and listens to all her husband's sermons. When the service ends,

---

17 Van Dernoot Lipsky, 6.
18 Van Dernoot Lipsky, 6.

she quickly joins her husband in the back to shake hands with parishioners. She even has several of her own ministries. Many parishioners view her as a very powerful, respected, and honored woman.

Pastor Steve, Julie's husband, is well liked by the parishioners. The sanctuary is always packed with people who come to hear his sermons and seem to believe that he is the greatest thing to ever happen to the church. Since he arrived, attendance is booming and good things are happening.

But there are a lot of secrets. In the parsonage Julie finds herself hiding when her husband is "in a mood." Steve has not hit her, but he has damaged plenty of other things. Once he took all the family photos off the wall and threw them down the hallway. She thinks it was because he decided that no one in the family respected him, but she has difficulty remembering all the details from that night. When he starts throwing things, her brain gets fuzzy. Now, every time she walks by the last photo in the row, she notices that there is still a crack in the glass, a reminder of his anger.

One day, Julie decided she wanted to make Steve happy. If she could make him happy, she knew the night would go smoothly. She fixed an amazing meal that required investing a couple hours, and she was excited for him to enjoy it. Unfortunately, Julie has experienced Steve complaining about her cooking and teasing her about not being as good of a cook as his mother, but she is confident this meal would not get that reaction. She finally feels as if she had done enough to pacify him for the night.

Steve walks in and smells the meal. He makes a face. Julie's heart sinks. She sets dinner out on the table, and Steve says, "I'm not eating this food" and promptly throws his plateful in the trash. He grabs a sports drink and heads to his office with a bag of potato chips. Julie bursts into tears. After a quick cry and even faster cover up, Julie pulls herself together, makes two plates, covers them with foil, and heads to her friend Sarah's house.

Sarah is a single woman who sits on the board, leads Vacation Bible School every year, and might need an extra home-cooked meal. Julie knows she will enjoy it, and just maybe Julie will find the courage to tell Sarah about what is happening at home.

Sarah and Julie sit down to eat together, and Julie tries to tell Sarah about Steve. But Sarah brushes it all off. "It's not right to talk about your husband like that," Sarah insists.

Julie feels even more discouraged and goes home. Sarah is now the sixth person in her faith community whom Julie has tried to talk to about this. She might as well give up. This is her life now. This is what she chose when she said her vows. If no one believes her, she is probably just making it up, and it is all in her head. Besides, Steve really is a great guy.

Discouraged, she crawls into bed, only to find Steve insisting that it's his right as her husband to get sex. She would rather do anything else but caves in because she knows if she does not, things will be even worse for her. There are too many precious items in the house, like her late grandmother's glass figurine. She would rather cave in now than watch it or something else get slammed into the wall.

The next day is the pastor and spouse retreat. You arrive to the event as a fellow pastor and notice Julie looks defeated. Her spunk is gone, and when you ask her what is wrong, she says she has a headache. You also notice her body is turned away from Steve's, as if she is terrified of him. Then you see her eyes are baggy, as if she has cried for days on end. Something is not right. You know it.

1. What do you do?
2. What sorts of things can you say to Julie to help her talk to you? To let her know that if she has a story to tell, you will believe her and respond to her, unlike the last six people?

3. What do you recommend happen to Pastor Steve? Does he deserve to be the leader of a large congregation? How can he be held accountable?
4. How safe do you think Julie is in this situation? How do you know?

Pastor/Expert Q & A

Pastor Samuel: My biggest question is in regard to maintaining healthy and safe boundaries while also being open and available. How does a pastor create healthy boundaries so not as to give fuel to the abusive spouse and also be able to be on vacation?

Expert: I think this is a great two-part question. First, let's tackle the part about vacation. Victims do not choose to leave at the exact moment we are available. They tend to leave when they fear for their life, and that might be when we are on vacation. My guess is you have an unwritten policy for what you would do if someone died or was critically ill during your vacation. Whatever that is, do the same for trauma moments of violence. For example, when I was a pastor, if a board member died on my day off, it would no longer be my day off. There are some things for which we let go of a vacation day without second thought. Death is one of these things. Another one of those situations is when someone is in extreme trauma, either in illness or, in this case, running for their life after a violent incident. So now the question becomes, How do we know if it is serious enough for us to let go of our precious day off?

Here are some signs for how you will know it is extreme trauma and you are needed immediately:

- They cannot think logically.
- Their thoughts blur together, and they cannot finish sentences.
- They are not breathing normally.
- They are rocking.

- They repeat some sort of a tick over and over. They say something like, "I just want to . . ." over and over. Whatever it is they want, they seem stuck on it (example: "I just want to go home").

If it is an aftershock of trauma (not a behavioral response immediately following a violent incident), there are ways to be present while still being on vacation. For example, if you get a forty-two-page, single-spaced email describing everything that went wrong, you do not have to read it in its entirety. Skim it to get the main points and respond with an appropriate emoji or the simple message, "I'm sorry all this is happening. Know I care." When someone pours out that much, at least acknowledge it.

The other part of what I think you are asking is, How do we help the victim without giving more fuel to the abusive partner? This is also an excellent question. Nothing could be more horrific than learning that when we tried to help, we actually made things worse. I would say, follow the lead of the victim. They will know what to do and say to not upset their abuser. They are experts at it. They cannot control the abuser's reaction, but they've stayed alive and survived this for a long time. They know what to do and when to do it. Trust them.

Second, I would say there are many ways to support a person without being completely obvious but that still let the survivor know that you care and you are present. This is a moment to be creative. How can you show your support without causing more harm?

———

Pastor Joshua: How do I respond when the survivor tells me all the horrific things that happened to them?

Expert: Let me share an example of helping a woman who was recently out of a domestic violence situation. She was just starting to realize how horrific it was, so she talked about the horror. She began to analyze what happened. She described the terrible things that had happened repeatedly to her. As she talked about these horrible things, I began a process for her of helping her remember the pain, and I also helped her recall her strength. With these two components, she will begin the process of weaving both the agony and strength into a new narrative that combines the two.

Here is what I did:

1. I validated and believed it was horrific. Sometimes I even point out what was so bad. Example: "It is really terrible that he would force you to have sex with him and make you pretend like everything was fine. That is just horrific." By phrasing it that way I showed her several things:

- I heard her story. I remember the details.
- I feel the intensity of the narrative. I think it is horrific.
- I showed that I believe her story.
- I validated the story and her emotions associated with the story.

2. I reframed what she said. I pointed out the incredible strength it takes to live through something so terrible. I tried to find examples of that strength. I talked about how even though she's remembering and realizing how bad it was, I also see how strong and amazing she is. Here is an example.

She says: "I realized how I had to pretend everything was OK even when I wanted to throw up. I was sick, and I wasn't allowed to be."

I then say: "Wow. The strength to get through that is unbelievably amazing. You kept going even after you were assaulted."

By phrasing it this way, I did several things:

- I showed that I was a witness to her story, the bad and the good.

- I did not just say she was strong. I demonstrated and gave her concrete ways I saw her strength evident in the midst of horror.
- I was sincere and honest. I did not make something up. I really saw a strength.

Why do I do this? As she is healing from sexual assault and violence at the hands of someone who promised to love and cherish her, she needs us (her spiritual leaders) to bear witness to the horror and bear witness to the strength (even when we have to point it out), so that eventually she can weave this into a new narrative. As she heals, her memory of the past will combine both the horror and her strength. This is important, and it is our responsibility as faith leaders to walk with her through this. With survivors of chronic trauma (like intimate partner violence or repeated sexual assault), I have to do this several times. When a person comes out of chronic trauma, their brains and bodies respond differently. It will take several cycles of this process, and I have to be patient and participate each time. Chronic trauma changes how we as faith leaders respond and support.

———

Pastor Jessie: How do I help someone deal with the fact that even though they've been trained, they didn't see the signs of abuse right in front of them?

Expert: It is so hard to confront abuse, and it is even harder to know the signs of violence only to learn it was happening right in front of you, and you had no idea. It is an unimaginable grief and pain. Especially when that abuse is happening to someone you love. The first thing you want to think is, How did I not know?

In 2017 a victim advocate who was my friend, whom I knew from state events, whom I talked to on the phone, and with whom I trained was murdered by her boyfriend. A victim advocate was killed by the very thing we all work to end, and it was devastating. We lost one of our own. It goes to show that violence can happen to anyone. There are no boundaries or limitations for who is violated and assaulted. It can happen to a victim advocate who herself knows all the signs of violence and actively works to end assault. It can happen to those of us who know the signs. It can happen to people we love. It can happen to anyone.

The violence is not about who it happens to; it is about the person who chooses to act violently. The best thing we can do in these situations when someone we care about is criticizing themselves for missing abuse right under their nose is to validate the person's abilities and gifts. They are still a valid and worthy person. They can still spot abuse in other situations. Abusers are sneaky, and we do not always see it. Also, victims tend to do everything to hide it (I know because I did). Sometimes we just cannot see it, and sometimes it takes someone we love to help us see. It is not fair, and it is terrifying to confront this reality.

Pastor Jessie: How does the community hold someone accountable for what they did?

Expert: I think one of the most brilliant things I have seen a faith community do to hold an offender accountable was what they did when they found out a woman was filing a protection order. They had some people stay with the woman while they waited for the courts to serve papers, and they had a team of people (whom the husband regularly spent time with) go be with him when he was served. When he found out he had been caught in extensive violence, the church community was there saying, "This is not acceptable behavior, and we are going to make sure it does not happen to her now." But it was done in a loving way, a way that said, "We are here and present."

I highly recommend *not* calling out the person in public. That is the least helpful thing you can do for the victim. If the survivor ends up going back at any point, public humiliation of the offender could set the victim up for more violence. I think the message needs to be communicated frequently in general—we do not tolerate the mistreatment of women and children, and we will hold you accountable.

Top 10: Are You Ready to Deal with Violence and Assault?

There are certain things a person must be willing to do before they are able to help a survivor of violence. This analysis seeks to evaluate and determine if leaders are ready to deal with the intensity of abuse.

1. First, we must be willing to let go of needing to feel good while dealing with victims and survivors. Violence is so horrific that, at any point in the process, it could feel as though you are on your first death call.

2. We must be willing to embrace pain and be vulnerable. When working with victims, one must be willing to admit there is abuse and be willing to feel it with the person. This includes letting the victim be vulnerable and realizing you are unable to control all the hurt.

3. We must be willing to be present, to become a person who can be seen, experienced, and touched. This is the birthplace of true empathy.

4. We must be ready to deal with what the abuser and violence reveal about ourselves: that we, too, have a capacity for evil, just like the offender. Abusers are not monsters running the streets, looking like beasts. They are human, just like us. When we realize another human has the capacity for this kind of violence, we must also be willing to confront the notion that we are capable of that violence too.

5. We must be able to genuinely connect with people as human beings with faults and annoyances. They are not a situation; they are a person.

6. We must accept people as they are and where they are. The hard truth about victims of chronic violence is that it will probably look as if they are messing up frequently. It is incredibly difficult to start life anew after having no control over your choices. Once a victim has freedom, chances are that they will not make entirely good choices every time—or for that matter, choices of which a good church person would approve. This is the process of learning how to use agency again. It takes time.

7. We must be able to see beauty within a person, even when many people just think the survivor is a scattered person who seems not to be able to make it in the world. Anyone who works with victims of violence must have penetrating vision. Once the survivor's "sea legs" are a bit more stable, their potential, which was always there, will come out again. But we all need people with the vision to see who survivors can be, in spite of experiencing trauma, and encourage them toward that vision.

8. We must be able to control ourselves from inactivity or overactivity. Both extremes could be as dehumanizing to a victim of domestic violence as the batterer's cycles of abuse. The victim must know you are present and care, but they must also know you have empowered them with control over their own life.

9. We must believe in ourselves to work with victims. It is hard work. If you do not believe in your own strength, you cannot show another person their power.

10. We must put aside what we want to do and say and hear what the victim wants to do and say.

5

Community Partners

One day I received a call from a survivor who was exasperated with her faith community. She described how she needed her pastor's help with paying some bills while she lived in a shelter and described how the pastor was calling this shelter, demanding to talk with someone working with her. He left voicemails with the staff, asking for updates and inside information. If the church was going to invest in helping pay her bills, he wanted to speak to someone at the shelter.

I was torn as I listened to her describe this situation because I could understand the pastor's side; he wanted to help in the best way possible. This minister probably had people holding him accountable and needed certain justification for spending church money. But I was mortified because, from the service provider side, he was violating every standard of confidentiality. The service provider was put in a corner, because if they want to keep their grant money, they need to follow confidentiality and could not respond to this pastor. But they also knew not responding could cost their client financial assistance and make things even more difficult.

I was also disturbed because the survivor herself was forced into a tough spot: if she wanted her bills paid, she had to comply with what the pastor wanted. The minister was demanding that she let him talk to the staff, even though this is not what she wanted. Thus, this became an ethical dilemma for the service provider, watching the pastor force the survivor to sign away her confidentiality rights so she could get help with her bills. The whole situation was a huge mess that could have been dealt with better if the faith community understood the roles of their community partners and respected basic confidentiality laws. The pastor held the power here, and instead of empowering the survivor, he demanded the power. He held the financial key to making sure this survivor kept her living space while she stayed safe before the trial, and although he may have needed information to report where funding was going, he did a lot of damage.

In this situation, the service provider was unable to spell it out for the pastor, and the survivor certainly was not in a place to explain the situation. Thus, I offer this chapter in the hope that these kinds of experiences for survivors improve. When domestic violence and sexual assault enter the church doors, several community partners will be involved, and it is important for the church leaders to know their role, understand when to refer, and understand when to let go of control.

I know pastors and faith leaders want to meet the needs of their people (and we all admire this compassion), but some situations are severe and extremely high-risk, and it is inappropriate for church leadership to handle them or make demands for inside information. When it comes to domestic violence and sexual assault, there are important things for clergy to do, crucial things for members of the church community to express, and essential things to be provided by professionals in this field. Both the secular and sacred have important roles for providing care for survivors.

This chapter will address understanding the community partners who work in the field of domestic violence and sexual assault and will analyze the Christian organization in relationship to the civic agencies. Standards of care will be addressed, explanations for who holds certain responsibilities will be given, and you will learn about confidentiality issues.

Standards of Care in the Secular Community

There are certain working assumptions and guidelines under which the secular community operates. These standards are expected to be met by the secular service providers. Some of these are based on grant requirements and are federal law. All of these requirements are based on what is considered best practices for providing trauma-informed care. These expectations may not line up with the values and beliefs of the local faith community, but it is very important to respect the required ethic of the service providers in your area.

The Department of Justice has several offices that are connected to it including the Office of Victims of Crime (OVC) and the Office of Violence Against Women (OVW).[1] Federal money goes from these offices to the state programs. The state then distributes the funding to local programs. Any agency connected to provisions from these offices must adhere to certain standards of care for victims.

The grant funding that community partners receive may vary. Most service provider programs receive federal funding, such as the Violence Against Women Act (VAWA) Funding,[2] Victims of Crime Act (VOCA) Funding,[3] and Family Violence Prevention

---

1   For more information about grants from the Office of Violence Against Women, see U.S. Department of Justice, OVW Grants and Programs, updated July 16, 2018, www.justice.gov/ovw/grant-programs.

2   For more information about VAWA grants, see U.S. Department of Justice, OVW Grants and Programs, updated July 16, 2018, www.justice.gov/ovw/grant-programs.

3   For more information about VOCA grants, see Office of Justice Programs, Office for Victims of Crime, Grants and Funding, https://ovc.gov/grants/types.html.

and Services Act (FVPSA), receive funding established by federal law and administered through various federal agencies.[4] If your local partners receive money from any of these agencies, you can assume they are required by federal law to meet certain conditions. For example, confidentiality is a requirement from the grantor and written in federal legislation.

All of these funding sources are absolutely critical to continue to provide abused persons safe shelter, transitional housing, safety, advocates, and more, so we need our service providers to follow these requirements. Many of these grants are formula grants that require a certain percentage be allocated to law enforcement, some to victim services, some to state prosecution, some to courts, and usually a small (or zero) percentage is discretionary.

There are many standards of service provision that I have encountered in secular and civic spaces. Note most of these involve showing respect for and acknowledging the basic human dignity of all persons, at all times, and adopting these standards could be helpful in the faith space too.

1. Confidentiality is maintained.

Disclaimer: Follow your state laws, be familiar with them, and know they change.[5] Know also that some states have very strict confidentiality laws and others have a bit more wiggle room. However, federal law trumps state law. So even if a state law allows sharing some information, VAWA halts it.

---

4   For more information about FVPSA, see the Family and Youth Services Bureau web page, www.acf.hhs.gov/fysb/programs/family-violence-prevention-services.

5   This entire section leans heavily on Alicia Aiken's webinar for the Battered Women's Justice Project titled "Respecting Information—Sharing Norms across Disciplines" from November 20, 2015. Available to view at https://vimeo.com/146944605.

There are ethical and legal responsibilities to keep confidentiality regarding the personal information for victims of crime. If a professional is privileged (for example, some states have advocate privilege; some do not), no one can make you share someone's personal information.

To respect someone's privacy is to respect their information is theirs and theirs only.

CONFIDENTIALITY involves the ethical responsibility to protect a person's identifiable information. Confidentiality maintains the information belongs to the person and the person only. It is not anyone else's to share.

Various legal acts (and subsequent grant allocation) guide what is done by community partners, including confidentiality. Three of them are very important for service providers involving domestic violence and sexual assault. These are: the Violence Against Women Act (VAWA), the Family Violence Prevention and Services Act (FVPSA), and the Victim of Crimes Act (VOCA).

Here are the most important pieces of these acts, especially as they relate to confidentiality:

VAWA (VIOLENCE AGAINST WOMEN ACT)[6]

VAWA is incredibly important federal legislation that originally passed in 1994 as a crimes law. It expired and was reauthorized in 2013. VAWA has been in effect in its current form since October 1, 2013. There have been additions made to this law, including protections for an expanded underserved population base.

---

6   The legislation is available to view at the Pennsylvania Coalition Against Domestic Violence web site, www.pcadv.org/Public-Policy/Laws-And -Regulations/.

a. *General Description:* These requirements are intended to ensure safety for victims. VAWA reads: "In order to ensure the safety of adult, youth, and child victims of domestic violence, dating violence, sexual assault, or stalking, and their families, grantees and subgrantees under this title shall protect the confidentiality and privacy of persons receiving services."

b. *What Cannot Be Shared:* "any personal identifying information"; "individual information collected in connection with services requested utilized, or denied"; "individual client information without the informed, written, reasonably time-limited consent of the person."

c. *If There Is a Court Order:* You must make "reasonable attempts to provide notice to victims" and "take steps necessary to protect the privacy and safety of the persons affected by the release of information."

d. *What Can Be Shared:* "nonpersonally identifying data"; "court-generated information"; "law-enforcement generated information"; "law enforcement- and prosecution-generated information."

Note: This means that what can be shared are things like statistics. However, even this would be restricted in a small town where identifying factors would make it easy to identify the person you are talking about; for example, when there is only one thirty-four-year-old Asian woman in the community.

FVPSA (FAMILY VIOLENCE PREVENTION AND SERVICES ACT)[7]

FVPSA is important legislation that was designed to shape how we treat people who are victims of family violence; it was first

7   The legislation is available to view at the Pennsylvania Coalition Against Domestic Violence web site, www.pcadv.org/Public-Policy/Laws-And-Regulations/.

authorized in 1984. Much of VAWA's content is based on the work of FVPSA.

a. *General Description:* "In order to ensure the safety of adult, youth, and child victims of family violence, domestic violence, or dating violence, and their families, grantee and subgrantees under this title shall protect the confidentiality and privacy of such victims and their families."

b. *What Cannot Be Shared:* "any personally identifying information" and "personally identifying information without the informed, written, reasonably time-limited consent by the person about whom information is sought."

c. *If There Is a Court Order:* You must "make reasonable attempts to provide notice to victims" and "take steps necessary to protect the privacy and safety of the persons affected by the release of the information."

d. *What Can Be Shared:* "Nonpersonally identifying information" and "court-generated information and law enforcement-generated information" and "law enforcement- and prosecution-generated information."

VOCA (Victims of Crime Act)

VOCA is funding for victims of crime, which includes domestic violence and sexual assault. It includes important information regarding confidentiality:[8] No recipient shall "reveal any information about a client that could be identified as any specific person."

Know that if a service provider is receiving any of the funding sources discussed here, they are expected to follow these legal requirements. This means, even if you are a pastor, you are not privileged to reveal or receive private information.

---

8   The legislation is available to view at the Pennsylvania Coalition Against Domestic Violence web site, www.pcadv.org/Public-Policy/Laws-And -Regulations/.

2. Service provision is for all, regardless of race, gender, sexuality, ethnicity, or any other factor.

There is often a focus on underserved populations for service providers. There may even be certain protections in place to help provide adequate services to meet the unique needs of various cultures, gender identities, or other factors.

3. Service provision is culturally appropriate.

Service providers want to make every attempt to meet culturally appropriate needs of their clients. This could include everything from food or dietary needs or even religious practices (even if they are different from their own).

4. Every attempt is made for the survivor to be safe physically and emotionally.

To be physically safe is for the body to be safe in space (perhaps a secret location for shelter). To be emotionally safe is to provide the type of space that allows for autonomy and agency (without causing harm to another's need for autonomy and agency).

5. Services are provided in a survivor-centered manner.

When services are survivor centered, they are offered primarily with survivors of traumatic violence in mind.

6. Privilege is given to survivors' voices, and services are provided based on information received from survivors.

Services are known to change based on need. Service providers are expected to listen to the needs of those in their community and respond accordingly. Many of the grants require surveys be given to service provision recipients to monitor care received. Those grants often push the grant recipient to show how the surveys are shifting service provision.

7. Trauma-informed care is a priority.

To be trauma informed is to know how trauma affects the body and brain of a person. How a service provider responds will be based on their understanding of the trauma response.

8. Services are free, without cost to the victim.

This is where grant funding comes into place. Service providers receive funding from the government to provide care to victims of crime. This ensures that victims can receive support during their entire system process (from court advocacy to safe shelter). All of this is provided through the grants mentioned above.

9. Services are voluntary, and survivors can drop services at any time.

Once a person begins receiving services from a civic provider, they are in no way obligated to continue to receive services. A well-trained service provider should know there is absolutely no way a requirement can be placed on service provision. For example, it should not be permitted for a service provider to require a person attend an event in order to receive services. All services should be accessed voluntarily and without any pressure to the person seeking services.

10. Services are provided in a respectful way that maintains the dignity and autonomy of the survivor.

The best service providers work to enable survivors to have as many choices and power over their circumstances as possible and provide services with respect and dignity.

11. Services are available to all, regardless of language, disability, literacy, and beyond.

Most service providers will have access to a language line. For this tool, a person calls the language line, an interpreter answers, and the survivor is able to receive services as if they spoke the primary language of the organization.

12. Service providers are to consider the intersectionality of many issues.

For example, service providers are asked to consider the intersection of race/ethnicity and violence or to consider the intersection of misogyny and violence. There are many other intersections, and service providers are asked to keep this at the forefront.

Many of the basic standards of how community agencies provide care are done in a way that values the human person. They are designed for survivor safety and are best care practices.

Getting to Know Community Partners and Their Roles

Many community partners are actively involved in helping a survivor of violence. Here is a brief summary of who would be the key players in your coordinated community response to assault and violence:

1. Law Enforcement

Police officers' role is to maintain order, enforce the law, respond to crisis, and minimize threat. They are a crucial piece of the criminal justice system. Although there are many kinds of police officers and persons in law enforcement, it is *not* their primary goal to be compassionate and kind and care for victims. That is the role of advocates. Many police departments employ a victim advocate on staff.

2. The Prosecutor's Office

Prosecutors (often called district attorneys, state attorneys, or solicitors) are key to the prosecution of deadly and harmful crimes. Often there will be a domestic violence unit or sexual assault crimes unit within the office. For example, my prosecutor's office has a domestic violence unit with several assistant district attorneys and several prosecutors. Their goal is to prosecute (and represent the state) in cases of domestic violence, in the criminal court system.

My neighboring prosecutor's office has a sexual crimes against children unit, again with several assistant district attorneys and prosecutors. Their goal is to prosecute (and represent the state) in cases of child sex crimes, in the criminal court system. Each prosecutor's office is often unique in organization and name.

3. Domestic Violence Shelters

The address of this community service provider is rarely known or shared. Usually a post office box is used, and calls are highly screened. The various staff positions at a shelter might be:

- Overnight staff
- Counselors
- Advocates
- Twenty-four-hour hotline staff

4. Domestic Violence Service Providers

Sometimes this includes a shelter; sometimes it does not. It depends on the program and its particular mission. Many times there are various advocates and staff housed at their location. For example, they may have a court advocate, a counselor, a victim advocate, a housing advocate, or a chaplain on staff.

5. Sexual Assault Service Providers

Some sexual assault service providers will be connected to domestic violence relief. We call those "dual service providers," and they meet the needs of those who are sexually assaulted (whether in the home or not) and those who are victims of domestic violence.

Sexual assault providers tend to have several therapists on staff. Sometimes the Sexual Assault Nurse Examiner (or even the forensic exam location) is housed in the same space as the sexual assault service provider (rather than the hospital). We often see that sexual assault service providers have a public location if there is no shelter attached.

6. Sexual Assault Nurse Examiner (SANE)

Sexual Assault Nurse Examiners are a group of nurses who are specially trained to administer the forensic exam to those who come seeking medical services after sexual assault. As was previously mentioned, sometimes these forensic collection rooms are located in a sexual assault service provider and sometimes they are located in hospitals.

The forensic exam can be an excruciating process. Victim advocates should be present or available to walk with the person through the exam that is administered by the SANE. The SANE collects evidence but has the primary concern of caring for the patient. The advocate's purpose is to care for the victim and family, not to collect evidence or offer legal advice.

Victims should *not* be required to pay for the forensic exam. This should be a provision of either the hospital, service provider, or criminal justice system.

Note that in the forensic exam:

- There is a box kit that is sealed with items to be used in the exam.
- Clothes will often be taken as evidence collection.
- Sometimes patients will be asked to do extraordinary things but know that they are not required to agree. These are things like taking hair samples from the root and can be quite painful.
- The exam can often take up to two hours.
- It is not best practice to call the forensic exam a "rape kit."

- The chain of command is extremely important for the exam. The nurse will stay with the box kit at all times until it is handed off to law enforcement.
- The amount of time after a sexual assault incident that evidence collection is possible is increasing substantially. At the 2017 National Sexual Assault Conference, it was estimated that latest research shows there is evidence present past 96–120 hours.
- There is no time limit after which a person who has been assaulted should be discouraged from seeking the medical care provided in the forensic exam.

7. Victim Advocates

COURT ADVOCATE

Court advocates walk with victims through the criminal justice process. There are often advocates on staff at the service provider and advocates on staff for the prosecutor's office. Both have different roles.

MEDICAL ADVOCATE

Medical advocates walk with victims through anything medical. For domestic violence this could mean assisting with dental appointments (as this is often a trigger).

PERSONAL ADVOCATE

Personal advocates walk with people as they personally process the act of crime committed against them. This might involve connecting a victim to the proper networks, and it might involve safety planning for victims still at risk.

LAW ENFORCEMENT ADVOCATE

This advocate will be present while the victim meets with law enforcement. The goals of the police and advocates are very different. The police need to work toward solving a crime and bringing justice, and advocates are there to be present for the victim through this overwhelming process.

PARENT/CHILD ADVOCATE

Often domestic violence agencies will have an emphasis on parent/child advocacy because they realize the strain on the protective parent (the one who is trying to protect the child and themselves from an abuser) and the child. This entire situation of violence against the parent (or the parent and child) creates an entirely different dynamic and problem. Domestic violence agencies tend to be at the forefront of meeting the needs created from those problems.

YOUTH ADVOCATE

Youth advocates focus on children and youth. The needs of those under eighteen are vastly different from adults, so youth advocates focus on meeting those specialized needs.

8. Community Educators

Community educators are present at community events to educate the public about issues of domestic violence and sexual assault. You might see them at:

- Health fairs
- Middle schools/high schools
- Colleges (addressing issues of campus sexual assault)

When to Refer

It is important to understand that each of the community partners has a role, and faith leaders are no exception. Faith leaders are not law enforcement, prosecutors, judges, trauma therapists, or any of the other key players in the system. Faith leaders have their own unique role. Just as we cannot expect a police officer to be a court advocate for a victim or expect a prosecutor to become a personal advocate, faith leaders cannot assume their master of divinity or faith leader training has prepared them for any of these community roles.

There are certainly times when we might immediately know we need to refer. Usually pastors tend to know they are not equipped to deal with someone with schizophrenia. However, faith leaders tend to think they can deal with all the pieces involved in the domestic violence and sexual assault experience, and this just is not true.

Here are a few examples of situations in which the pastor or faith leader should be on alert to refer:

1. *Trauma healing.* Refer to a specialized trauma counselor who understands the body and brain in trauma and is trained in tools to facilitate the healing process.
2. *Safety.* When it comes to safety planning and safe shelter, refer to your local provider. You can provide minimal emergency safety planning, but it is crucial to have the person talk to someone who is well versed in safety needs. You are also not equipped to provide safe housing. Refer to your local provider.
3. *Legal advice.* It is usually considered an ethical violation for someone without legal training to offer legal advice. It can also be illegal. If you give legal advice as a minister, you could be charged with practicing law without a license. Remember that pastors and faith leaders (regardless of their personal experience) are not attorneys. Leave the legal advice to those trained and equipped to deal with family court, criminal court, and all the needs therein.
4. *Twenty-four-hour access.* Twenty-four-hour hotlines are employed by multiple people in any given twenty-four-hour period. They are equipped and prepared to deal with crisis. However, this is *not* to say that when a victim really

needs you it is acceptable to brush them off. This situation involves a fine line and a delicate balance. Pastors and faith leaders seem to have a hard time distinguishing between extreme threat and immediate need and an ongoing crisis that requires twenty-four-hour support. Do not miss the extreme threat and immediate need. It could cause more harm.

The United States national twenty-four-hour hotlines are always available.

- Phone: 1-800-799-7233
- Phone TTY: 1-800-787-3224
- Phone in Spanish: 1-800-799-7233
- 24-hr bilingual domestic violence helpline: 651-772-1611 (from Casa Esperanza)
- Website (with an online chat available): www .thehotline.org/. For Youth: www.loveisrespect .org/. Text: loveis to 22522

5. *Enforcement of Protection Orders and Safety Measures.* Do not expect to be able to enforce a protection order, even if you know the offender. Keep the protection order *on file* in the church's office, but do not expect to enforce it. The church simply has it on record for a police officer's use.
6. *Victim Advocacy (beyond personal and spiritual support).* Can you go to court with a victim? Of course. Are you the court advocate? Absolutely not. Can you recommend an agency? Yes. Can you drive them to shelter? Absolutely not. Can you check in with them on their cell phone? Yes, of course. Can you call the shelter and ask about their progress? Absolutely not. Know the line and the boundaries, and do not violate them.

So, what role does the faith leader have when it comes to domestic violence and sexual assault? The church leader providing pastoral care to survivors is providing spiritual care and guidance during trauma and crisis. This means there are several roles and responsibilities that are in the church's power. Some of these are listed below and offer guidance on what to watch out for and not do; others are things to make sure you are practicing.

The Church's Roles and Responsibilities

1. Be informed about when law enforcement and first responders need to be called onto the scene.
2. Be comfortable with silence.
3. Check your own triggers (see chapter 5).
4. Understand the complexities of chronic trauma, trauma responses, and the effect on the body (see chapter 2).
5. Know your limits and boundaries. Have a self-care plan (see chapter 5).
6. Err on the side of believing that violence or abuse really did take place (see Appendix I for more information about the likelihood of false reporting).
7. Put aside the desire to be a theodicy expert on why bad things are happening.
8. Watch your theology, especially as it relates to forgiveness, divorce, or "time heals all wounds."
9. Practice active listening. Be present in the moment, and hear the cries of the survivor.
10. Know the difference between connecting and understanding versus trying to solve the problem or explain it.
11. Make offender accountability a priority.
12. Never suggest couples counseling where there are issues of power and control.
13. Remember that behaviors of victims tend to be paradoxical and not make sense. The behavior is not the main problem; it is a symptom. Violence is the problem.

Remember, if you are ever concerned or unsure of when to refer, contact your local service provider. In my experience, most domestic violence and sexual assault agencies are happy to work with a willing and respectful church community. There are some cases where it would be in the survivor's best interest to allow you to share identifying information with another and the survivor wants you to share this information. In these cases, a confidentiality waiver is highly recommended.

If you use a confidentiality waiver, it is important to understand the following:

1. The survivor can start to read/sign the document and immediately change their mind. If they do, you must respect their wishes.
2. The survivor must understand they are signing away their right to have otherwise protected information shared now by you.
3. The waiver should be no less than fifteen minutes and no more than fifteen days. Some standard forms may go to thirty days, but I recommend fifteen days.
4. The information released must be specific, and you cannot share anything that is not listed.
5. This document helps protect both the survivor and the church. This helps the survivor understand exactly what about their information is shared and helps them think through why they might want it shared. They also have complete control over what is shared. This document helps the church by not sharing any information a person does not wish to be shared and saves the community from potential legal disasters by sharing information that was personal and confidential.

Sample Confidentiality Waiver Agreement

(Note: Use appropriate church letterhead.)[9]

I, _____ (name of survivor), understand that _____ (church's name) has a responsibility to keep my private and personal information, identifying factors, and records confidential.

I also understand that I have a choice to allow _____ (church's name) to share some or part of my private, personal information, identifying factors, and records.

I authorize _____ (church's name) to share this specific information about me. (Be as specific as possible.)

Who I want to have my information: _____
Agency: _____
Phone Number: _____

(Circle one or more):

This information can be shared: In person / On the phone / Hard-copy mail / Email (and I understand electronic mail cannot be kept confidential as it can be intercepted and read by others).

The reason I want this information shared is because: (be as specific as possible)

(Know that there is a risk that a limited release of information can potentially open up access by others to all of your confidential information.)

I understand:

---

9   This confidentiality waiver is based on the work by the Network to End Domestic Violence, the national Domestic Violence Coalition (NNEDV). For the original recommendation, see https://docs.google .com/viewerng/viewer?url=https%3A%2F%2Fnnedv.org%2F%3 Fis-google%3D8183&hl=en&mdocs-session=8dde27559b09f170642 d9e40fd26ba99.

1. I do not have to sign a release form for _____ (church's name).
2. Releasing information about myself could let others know about my location.
3. _____ (church's name) may not be able to control the information once they release it.

This release expires:

_____ (Date); _____ (Time)

(Note: This should be no less than fifteen minutes and no more than fifteen days.)

I understand this confidentiality release is valid upon signing it, and I can withdraw my consent to this release at any point.

Signed: _____

Date: _____ Time: _____

Witness Signature: _____

Protection Orders Demystified

A protection order is a legal document issued from the court, intended to provide incentive that one party not harm another. When a person is abused, mistreated, or violated by another, they may petition a judge for such an order.

Here are the basics of protection orders:

Filing the Initial Order

- In order to receive a protection order, a person must go to the courthouse and fill out the appropriate paperwork. At least one of the following must happen or be in the jurisdiction of the court: the incident(s), the residence of the applicant, or the residence of the offender. There is not usually a cost to file.
- The initial order is temporary, but a court date will be scheduled for both parties to be present and argue their

side. The courts will inform the second party of the temporary order and court date. The second party must be informed in order for there to be a hearing.

- If the judge signs the initial order, it is *ex parte*, meaning that it is an order issued for a short time without all persons involved present or represented. This means someone who is abused can request the order without their abuser present.
- *Due process* is a legal term indicating everyone has the right to fair treatment in the legal system. An *ex parte* order temporarily bypasses due process since one party is not present or represented to speak for themselves. If the judge grants the order, they determined the case was serious and lethal enough to bypass due process rights.
- If divorce and custody court proceedings are simultaneous to the protection order, hired attorneys will often work the final protection order into the divorce decree.
- After the temporary *ex parte* protection order, a court date will be set. The victim and abuser will have to go to court to argue their sides for a final order.
- In my experience, judges tend to want:

  1. *Specific and detailed instances.* In other words, "He abuses me all the time" is not an acceptable notation on the request. The judge would rather see: "On Sunday, October 12, at approximately 2:00 p.m., he grabbed my wrist, forcing me to stay in the room." List the most recent incidents first. Again, because an *ex parte* order temporarily violates the rights of a person, judges want to know why this is an urgent and present request.
  2. *Incidents that show threat to the physical body.* This can mean more than body-to-body contact. Physical violence is anything that involves the body: being trapped, having items thrown, and so forth.

3. *Clear proof and an adequate description.* Why does the person fear for their life, safety, and well-being?

4. *Documentation.* This can be in the form of emails, texts, doctor's records, and so forth.

- On the form for an *ex parte* protection order, you can expect to see commonalities, regardless of the state. Additional handwritten pages are usually acceptable. In some states, pets can be protected (as property).

- Often the abuser files a protection order and sneaks through the system, writing themselves into the victim role. In my experience, I have seen many victims feeling overwhelmed and horrified because they received an *ex parte* order against them. The victim cannot find the appropriate words and speak about what is happening, and the abuser is smooth, slick, and full of words that put them in the seat of the oppressed.

- Sometimes it is not the safest option for a person to file a protection order. Only the victim knows what is best for them. When a person leaves abuse, it is the most dangerous time, and filing an order can cause the abuser to become more violent and deadly. The bottom line is that we cannot force victims to file an order because we could be forcing them into a more dangerous situation.

The Hearing

- When both parties go to the courthouse for the hearing, the *plaintiff* is the one who filed the case, and the *defendant* is the one responding to the case. There should be signs and/or verbal instruction to indicate where you should sit in the courtroom.

- I highly recommend finding a domestic violence or sexual assault advocate who specializes in court advocacy. They will know your community's judges, attorneys, and process. Each county has various ways of doing things, and your local court advocate will know these pieces.

- As the court hearing begins, someone will announce that this is the docket for protection orders, and they will call every name scheduled that day. When the victim hears their name, they are to announce "present."

- When the plaintiff and defendant are called to the judge, each will be given time to talk about the situation. Usually if anyone is allowed to proceed forward with the two parties, it will be a court advocate. Witnesses may be called to share what they observed and experienced, but they do not usually approach the judge initially. There is no jury. Attorneys may or may not be present.

- In my experience, judges do not want to see the two parties speak to each other or argue. I have watched too many victims take the bait of abusers and lose it right there in front of the judge. The victim should expect to answer the judge's questions but not engage with the other party unless the judge instructs a response. The victim should be careful to never speak over the judge or the accused.

Top 10 Recommendations When Subpoenaed to Testify in Family Violence Cases

1. The less you say the better. Answer only the question asked. Do not volunteer extra information unless you think it is absolutely important. The attorneys will guide the questioning appropriately.

2. Think about wearing a business suit. This is the expected look in the courthouse for legal proceedings.

3. Do not be afraid to take a deep breath or take time to think. If you are confused, ask them to rephrase the question. If you need more time to think, restate what they just said by saying "What I hear you asking is x, is that correct?" This helps you gain time to process the question.

4. Do not be afraid to say, "I cannot speak to that. What I can speak to is *x*." This takes the conversation from where someone might be leading you to where it is in your control. If you do not know, tell them you do not know and cannot speak to that issue.
5. Be early. Get familiar with the space in which you will be questioned. Get your head in the space.
6. If you are going to the courthouse, be aware of what is on your person and in your bags. You will have to get through metal detectors. Sometimes even what is in your hair sets off the machines.
7. Come with grounding techniques for yourself. If you feel yourself panicking from the immensity of it all, start identifying colors or textures around you. It brings you back to the present. Or start doing math problems in your head or thinking of favorite quotes. That will bring you out of a panic and get your frontal-lobe cognition working.
8. Know that family court proceedings can be very nasty. Custody is messy. This will probably be difficult, if not grueling.
9. Remember your testimony is just a piece of the puzzle. The whole world does not fall on you. You are just speaking to one small aspect of a larger situation.
10. Make eye contact. Keep your shoulders back and head up. This is easy to forget in these overwhelming situations. Sometimes before I go in I do some yoga stretches. Then I do a Wonder Woman pose for a little while. Research shows putting your body in a stance of power helps your brain remember how strong you are and makes you feel more confident.

Case Study: Weapons in the House

Ashton is a high-level business executive who struggles with drugs and alcohol. It started in college while he was fighting to stay at the top of his class and become what he is today. Ashton is convinced he can control the problem, and no one thinks much of it. He has power and money so he is obviously doing just fine. Ashton is an avid sportsman and often brags about how many guns he has and what a good shot he is.

When Ashton drinks to relax or takes stimulants to stay up and finish a business proposal, he almost always ends up hurting his wife, Amy. You know this because one day she showed up with bruises all around her neck from where he had shoved a shotgun down her throat and threatened to blow her head off. No one in the church would ever imagine Ashton doing something so vile, but he did. Alcohol and drugs make his behavior even worse. He is also a high-paying tither, so the situation involves financial concerns for both the church and minister.

Amy wants to stay with Ashton. She insists she loves him and that if she could just do what he wanted her to do when he asked, there would not be any problems like this. She believes it is all her fault. Besides, Amy is a Christian who reads her Bible and studies her women's devotional faithfully. She learned that divorce is wrong, a sin even, and she refuses to take part in anything that could separate her from God.

1. What do you say to Amy?
2. What do you say to Ashton?
3. What do you do about the weapons in the house?
4. What is your recommendation?
5. How concerned are you about the tithe money?

Pastor/Expert Q & A

Pastor Christine: What do I need to know about the rape kit?

Expert: Ah, yes. The forensic exam. We call it a "forensic exam" instead of a "rape kit." Forensic exam is more descriptive of the procedure used in all forms of sexual assault. The kit is the actual box of items used to collect and store the evidence. For the forensic exam, a SANE (Sexual Assault Nurse Examiner) will meet with the victim to primarily provide healthcare and, secondarily, to collect evidence. SANEs are trained specifically for this task. Often a hospital or service provider will have several SANEs on staff, and they rotate who is on call. The goal is usually to be at the hospital or location within thirty to forty-five minutes of being called.

If there is not a SANE available in your town, the victim may have to travel a long distance or have an exam done by someone who is not specially trained. Neither of those options is ideal. Know that the evidence collection process can be overwhelming. Hair is plucked and tweezed, nails are swiped, body charts are drawn, questions are asked, swabs are used, and so much happens that it can take up to two hours to complete.

A victim advocate from your local service provider should be available to walk with the victim through the process. They will let you know things like:

- Clothes will be taken and cut (and they often have clothes for the survivor there to wear home).
- At any point during the exam, the victim can say they do not want to do this portion. They have that right. The victim has the control. For example, if they do not want their hair removed by the roots, they can refuse that part of the exam.
- The victim should not be the one to pay for the exam.

Pastor Christine: I have no idea what to do after the police report. I know I can help take her to file a police report, but how do I help her after this?

Expert: I think the fact that you're asking this question is a fantastic sign. You know your limits and when you need to refer. On that note, find your local service provider for information about what kind of help is offered in your area. If you want to find reputable and accredited ones in your area, I recommend searching the National Network to End Domestic Violence (NNEDV). This is the national coalition that can provide links to all the state coalitions.[10]

From the national coalition, find your state coalition (example: in Kansas, it is the Kansas Coalition Against Sexual and Domestic Violence, KCSDV) and then search for member services under their name.

The state coalitions tend to have a map or to be divided by county. Note that some states combine domestic and sexual violence and that some states have two coalitions—one for domestic violence and one for sexual assault (in Texas there is the Texas Association Against Sexual Assault, TAASA and the Texas Council on Family Violence, TCFV).

Once you find your state coalition, search for the accredited agencies that are members of that coalition. Usually only the best service providers are connected to coalitions. Those accredited agencies will be community organizations in your area. These providers tend to have free counseling services, group therapy, court advocacy, a twenty-four-hour hotline, and much more. Check out what services your local agency provides.

Pastor/Expert Q & A

Chaplain Ty: How can I support both sides of victimization? The abuse victim and the abuser's unknowing and shocked family?

Expert: That is a great question, especially in cases of sexual assault. Perhaps there is one person who violated another. The victim comes forward, and the perpetrator's family also feels victimized. In these situations, everything tends to feel wrong. We do not know who to help or how to balance it all.

---

10 The current link for the National Network to End Domestic Violence is: https://nnedv.org/content/state-us-s-territory-coalitions/.

The first and most important thing is that the faith leader's reaction is completely valid. This is an incredibly complex situation, and it is completely acceptable to feel overwhelmed and maybe even scared of what to do next. Second, because there are multiple layers of victimization, many reactions are possible. The perpetrator's family might not think they were violated (perhaps they do not believe the accusation), or they might feel overwhelmed and lost themselves. Whatever way they respond will determine how we walk alongside them. The important thing is to remember how we help them comes from where they are, not where we think they should be. Know that the family may need additional support outside of what you can provide.

The victim will need you but will require support in ways beyond a faith leader's tool kit. Be prepared to refer when necessary, but do not hand every piece of the situation off too quickly. As someone called to pastoral care, there is a spiritual component of walking alongside people in trauma we must keep in mind. Bear witness to the stories of pain and agony. Celebrate and point out the ways you see the strength of the survivor, and help them begin to integrate this into a new narrative.

Most of all, know that although you have an important role, everything does not fall on you. Seek out support from your community partners who are trained to deal with this. Contact your local sexual assault service provider and find out what they offer. There are probably resources you don't know about yet. Discover them.

6

Active Shooters and Other Family Violence Threats

One early Sunday morning I made my way through a church building with a mission in mind. I knew that my daughter was already in the children's section and was aware no one knew who I was. I was dressed well and professionally, and I lifted my chin high, ready to see how far I could go. My mission was this: Would I be able to get to my daughter without any interference from staff or a member of the church safety team? I would soon find out. With hope in my heart that the church community would not fail, I made my way over to the children's section and attempted to walk in unannounced and uninvited. I had absolutely no right to be there, and nothing indicated I should be permitted.

Because I understand the complexities of church safety, especially as it relates to family violence, I was relieved when a young man stopped me. He welcomed me to the church, greeted me warmly, and made sure I could not go any farther without chatting with him about who I was, where I was going, and what my intent was. Our exchange was entirely friendly, and had I not known what to look for, I probably would not have suspected that there was a plan in place to deal with a situation like this. It was brilliant.

It turned out this young man was on the church safety team. I could not sing his praises enough. There was nothing about me that should have indicated I would be dangerous, but he still stopped me. He was prepared, and he acted when he needed to act. However, he also acted in such a loving and welcoming way that I would have never known what he was doing. I simply felt welcomed and included.

Because I help train and lead church safety seminars, and my father helps to lead that particular team, my cover was quickly blown. However, that church got five gold stars from me. I wish every faith community had safety measures like this in place. Even though the church is supposed to be a safe place, a sanctuary, we cannot assume our churches will be always be safe. News reports of church shootings tell us that even the church can become the location of a mass shooting, just like a school, mall, or concert. Violence can creep into our doors and take the lives of our members and friends.

According to church security consultant Carl Chinn, from January 1999 through December 31, 2017, there were 1,705 deadly force incidents in faith-based organizations across the United States.[1] Of those 1,705 incidents, 616 people were killed, and 943 were injured.[2] If these numbers seem small to you (perhaps because there are hundreds of thousands of churches in the United States), know that as time passes, the numbers are increasing and the problem is growing. Prior to 1963, it is believed, there was never a mass murder on church property in

1 Carl Chinn, "Deadly force incidents (DFI) include 'abductions [& attempts], attacks, suspicious deaths, suicides & deadly force intervention /protection,'" Deadly Force Statistics, CarlChinn.com, updated January 14, 2018, http://nebula.wsimg.com/27ed2af7fc8143c90bb171 46ea743dfb?AccessKeyId=16B07A2D0672906279DB&disposition=0& alloworigin=1.

2 Chinn, www.carlchinn.com/.

the United States.[3] In 1999 there were 22 nonaccidental deaths on church property.[4] In 2009 the number more than doubled to 54 deaths in one year, and by 2017, there were 118 nonaccidental deaths in the faith space.[5] Unfortunately, deadly violence is a problem, even on church property.

When I train church safety classes with our police chief, sometime during the class our colleague, Ed Smith, asks the audience to bow their heads. He says, "Today we talked about some difficult things, and now we need to just take a moment and pray together." Sometimes he begins the Lord's Prayer. Other times a class participant will come up and begin to petition the divine for grace and mercy. But every single time, when the person who is praying gets about two sentences in, Ed pushes "play" on his machine. The sounds of what happened in one congregation blare through the room. We hear gunshots and screaming, crying, and fear; and the quiet moments of prayer are ruined.

I sit in the back and watch class participants. Inevitably, most of them have quite an extensive involuntary startle response. This is because prayer time is supposed to be safe. It is supposed to be a moment when we find sanctuary. Those moments of prayer were supposed to be a time when we took a break from dealing with the potential for violence and encountered God. Ed's point is this: Even in our faith communities, we cannot let our guard down. Vulnerable moments (like prayer) are "soft spots" that can become a place for threats.[6] He looks at the class intensely and solemnly declares, "Welcome to your new reality." Although it is a depressing thought, he is right. Violence can be prevented

3   Chinn, www.carlchinn.com/. To qualify as a mass murder, four or more people are killed.
4   Chinn, www.carlchinn.com/.
5   Chinn, www.carlchinn.com/.
6   The notion of "soft spots" originated with Dr. William (Edward) Smith, DT, in his training material on vulnerability during prayer and other instances.

and even stopped on church property if we face the fact that it is possible in our safe space and take steps to prepare for such an event. We can never become complacent, even on the holy ground of the church.

In this chapter you will find basic tools for preparing for a church crisis, including child custody issues and active shooters. As the 2017 Baptist church shooting in southern Texas made very clear, mass shootings in faith communities are, all too often, directly connected to family violence. Therefore, the book will end with tools and resources for preparing for an active shooter. As Chief Anthony Williams says: "If it is foreseeable, it is preventable."

Family Violence and Deadly Force Incidents

According to Carl Chinn, when a motive for a deadly force incident could be determined specifically in a church space, (1,282 of 1,660 cases), domestic violence accounts for 207 of the 1,282 and nonfamilial conflict accounts for 173.[7] The other top category is robbery, which is the most common church security issue. Another research group determined that of all the mass shootings that occurred between January 2009 and December 2016, "54 percent of mass shootings involved a partner or other close family member that was killed."[8] Whether we want to or not, faith communities must deal with the fact family violence creeps into the faith space and puts everyone at risk.

High-Risk Locations for Deadly Force Incidents

The place of highest risk for deadly force incidents is the parking lot. Again, Carl Chinn's research tells us that of the 1,705 deadly force incidents, 1,213 of those occurred in the parking lot or away

---

7   Training materials, Dr. William (Edward) Smith.
8   "Domestic Violence," Everytown for Gun Safety, accessed June 28, 2018, https://everytown.org/issue/domestic-violence/.

from the building.[9] The number decreases inside the building as 424 of those happened within the church walls.[10]

This information tells us that we have to be prepared for violence on our church property before people walk in the doors. Wise church leaders have someone monitoring the parking lot, adequate lighting, and are attentive to attendees before activities begin and after they end. We cannot control an active shooter, but we can control their opportunity to harm. We can control the door entry, implement policies, have trained safety teams, and have a plan.

Denominational Affiliation

Often there are denominations or faith groups that say, "This can never happen here." Thus, I think it is important to point out the churches where these deadly force incidents occurred.[11]

Denomination/Faith Community	Number of Deadly Force Incidents
Unknown/Unaffiliated	384
Baptist	367
Catholic	236
Methodist	115
Lutheran	63
Presbyterian	60
Islamic	34
Jewish	22
Nazarene	11
Buddhist	6

---

9   Chinn, www.carlchinn.com, http://nebula.wsimg.com/27ed2af7fc8143 c90bb17146ea743dfb?AccessKeyId=16B07A2D0672906279DB&dispo sition=0&alloworigin=1.

10 Chinn, www.carlchinn.com/.

11 Chinn, www.carlchinn.com/. Note that some of the incidents affected more than one denomination. Chart based on the research of Carl Chinn.

What this disturbing and disheartening list shows is that no matter what religion or denomination you are, it can happen to you.

Just Trust God

When I train with our police chief he demonstrates in our church safety classes how unhelpful it is to "just trust God." He picks the biggest guy in the class—you know, the one whose shoulders are the size of an average person's head. Then he chooses a small person, often a spunky but smaller woman. He brings them both to the front of class. Chief instructs the big guy to face him and lines up the tiny woman behind the big guy (so the man's back is to the woman). Chief instructs the man to cross his arms over his chest and tells him no matter what, he needs to trust that God will take care of him.

At this point the man's concern tends to become evident as he realizes what Chief is about to ask him to do. Then the tiny woman is asked to brace her arms up and get ready to catch the big man as he falls back. Chief reminds the man to trust God. He should have enough faith that God will protect him! And before they complete the exercise, Chief calls it off and releases the two volunteers to join the audience.

One of the church phrases I hear often is "Just trust God" or "God will protect us." The believer is passionate about how they will be safe in church because they have faith God will care for them. Although this seems to be a great thought, it can be problematic when thinking about family violence occurring on church property.

Logically, there is a problem with this idea. Does claiming God will protect us mean God did not protect the hundreds of people who have died on church property? Of course not. When we talk about our safety in terms of trusting God to protect us, what do we say when violence happens to us? Usually we try to push the blame elsewhere (evil, the shooter, and so forth), even though we said we trusted that God would protect us. This is not logical. Thus, we must rethink how we speak in the faith community about God's action regarding violence.

It is ridiculous to trust that God will protect you from something like falling backwards onto someone smaller than you, expecting they will catch you. The same is true about violence on church property. We can no more trust that God will protect our community from a violent incident than we can trust we won't fall on the ground in Chief's exercise. It is time to change how we view how the divine is expected to keep us safe, and instead take actions to keep people safe, as agents of God's love and care. This trust/fall exercise shows us that reality and just trusting God are very different. Family violence requires us to confront reality and deal with the potential for violence in our perceived safe spaces.

The Church's Responsibility for Safety on Church Grounds as It Relates to Family Violence

When it comes to family violence, the church has an ethical responsibility to ensure that children and families are safe while physically on the property. We must plan for crisis situations now, before there is a problem. If we can plan, think through, and prepare now, we can save lives and avoid lawsuits. This chapter will help you prepare your procedural memory (the most primitive part of your brain) so that when a crisis happens, you are prepared to deal with it adequately and efficiently.

The Ethical Responsibilities of the Church Community

1. *First and foremost, we must let go of the notion that "God is going to protect us"* so there will not be a serious issue in our space.[12] Even though it is tough to deal with and causes us pain,

---

12 Material in this section is created based on material for the class "Church Safety Training," designed and written by Marieta Oglesby, MLS, CCP, a member of the AIMS Training and Consulting Team. Other contributors include Chief Anthony Williams, Dr. William "Edward" Smith, DT, and Chaplain James Bradley, DCCCD PD.

we must deal with the fact that family violence happens to the people in our congregations and it often comes with them on our property.

2. *Keep protection orders, divorce decrees, and custody papers on file.* If there is a person who is being abused in your congregation who has filed a protection order, it needs to be kept safe on the church property. Why? Because if there is an incident on your property, this is the first thing law enforcement will ask to see. If there is record of a custody battle or court decisions regarding custody of children for a family in your church community, this paperwork must be kept safe on the church property. If the noncustodial parent comes to pick up the child and leaves, the church can be held at fault. Bottom line, if there are court orders, keep them on file.

However, remember that sharing a protection order without the written and explicit consent of the victim is a violation of confidentiality. Be sure to take care of this before others (even the safety team) are informed of this personal information.

3. *Identify a safe room.* One of the easiest and smartest things a faith leader can do is identify a room that would be safe for a victim if an incident happens. Think about this in advance. Where is a place on your church property to which you could take a threatened person?

4. *Establish safety teams from the pulpit to the parking lot.*[13] Safety teams seem to be an increasingly popular addition to faith communities, and this is a good thing. Utilize the resources already in your community. Do you have any active or retired military, law enforcement, security officers, or teachers in your congregation? What about someone from the fire department, a lawyer, facility managers, or counselors? Would any of them be willing to take turns being actively alert in the parking lot before

---

13 If you want to train your teams with the team I work with and Chief Anthony Williams, contact AIMS Consulting and Training, www.aims consulting-training.com/church-safety-seminars.html.

and after services? Think about how those who are already in your community can take an active part in keeping your community safe.

Safety teams should be informed of divorces and custody agreements or protection orders. If they are informed of this confidential and private information, a confidentiality waiver should be signed by the survivor. This team should also be trained on how to observe and recognize potential threats.

5. *Create procedures and policies for church safety.* The phrase "policies and procedures" tends to cause intense panic in the hearts and minds of faith leaders. And although it can feel overwhelming, there are resources available to help with this. On our team we have a person (Marieta Oglesby) who specifically trains on this and helps churches develop their own policy. When creating your procedures and policies, remember to:

    a. Have regular training for all staff and volunteers on domestic violence and sexual assault (in addition to child abuse). Contact your local shelter or service provider. Usually they have grant requirements to provide community education and presentations.

    b. Watermark drafts as drafts (so they are not used in court as final policy).

    c. Foster a community of trust so victims communicate when they do not feel safe.

    d. Decide at what point you will contact law enforcement or other community partners for help.

    e. Practice for an emergency. Are there exercises you can do with key members? Perhaps practice what someone would do to call 911.

    f. Find out if weapons are permitted on church property. Some states require signage with this decision.

    g. See if some of your community partners do a regular threat assessment, or survey the physical space with church safety in mind.

h. Decide what steps you will take when you witness unruly outbursts, yelling, threats, belligerence, hostility, or aggression. List them. First you will do this, second you will do this, and so forth.

i. Learn to be more culturally aware, and seek training in issues of diversity.

j. Determine who is responsible to do what and when they should do it.

k. Ask if everyone on the safety team and those leading classes knows the church address and phone number? Where is it posted?

l. Decide when background checks should be conducted.

m. Make an evacuation plan for use during a threat.

n. Determine your method for recognizing suspicious and potential threats.

o. Find out what doors are usually unlocked and when doors are unlocked and locked.

p. Know your limitations and when to refer.

q. Have a safety plan for custody issues.

r. Learn your state laws on conceal and carry. See if you have signs posted; ask if you need them in English and Spanish or another language, and make sure they are visible.

s. Decide where to post your evacuation plan.

The goal of designing policies and procedures about church safety is to be proactive and think about this now before you are reacting to a situation. The documents should be ever-evolving as time passes, and they should always be in writing. Remember this is also a legal issue. If you are sued, you can say "I did *x, y,* and *z,* in accordance with our policy." You are liable and can be sued for improper handling of these issues. The church can (and has been) sued for improper responses.

6. *Know that the "all are welcome" policy means anyone can come on your church grounds.* Because the church is a place for

everyone to find love and forgiveness, it becomes a place where anyone is welcome on your property. Remember also that the threats could come from within, not just from outside. We cannot assume what is out there is not also inside. Think through what this means for your space and your congregation.

7. *Realize your vulnerable spaces.* Think of the most vulnerable places, events, and people in your congregation. Funerals? Prayer? Youth spaces? Women's events? Men's Groups? Schools? When eyes are closed? Think through when people would be susceptible to threat.

8. *Have escorts to and from the parking lot.* When it comes to issues of family violence and intimate partner violence, consider having someone designated to walk to and from the parking lot with a survivor. The parking lot is the most dangerous place, and by simply thinking of this ahead of time and taking steps to mitigate the threat, lives can be saved.

9. *Remember that lights are the cheapest form of security.* I was raised by a state trooper, and I think I heard him say this phrase a million times. When I wrote this, I heard it in my head in his voice: "At all times, keep your church property lighted well. It is the cheapest form of security."

10. *Think through child pickup/drop off as it relates to custody issues.* I said this before, but it bears repeating. Think carefully about how you will keep children safe in your children's area. Who can pick up the child? Who has custody? Where are the custody papers located? Think through this now before it becomes a problem. Volunteers must be aware of the custody agreement and know who is responsible to pick up children and when.

11. *Make sure you have a central door for entry but all doors can be used as an exit.* Being able to exit a door from the inside that might be locked on the outside is an issue the fire department will usually point out to churches. However, having one entry with a team of people ready to greet at that one entry is a

wiser move for those knowing family violence can cause a potential threat.

Beyond these recommendations, know that church safety is an important issue to consider when thinking through how domestic violence and sexual assault affect our congregations and how we provide pastoral care in the midst of such situations. We have a responsibility to maintain spaces that consider safety now, before it becomes an issue. Issues of domestic violence, sexual assault, and family violence will creep into your congregation. The question is, How prepared are you to deal with all the complexities that come with it?

De-escalation Techniques: Practical Ways to Diffuse a Situation

There are times when you will be able to de-escalate a situation before it becomes too intense. Here are some recommendations for this:

- Stop and think. Do not respond, and do not speak right away. Think for five seconds. Do not react with your primitive brain even though it is tempting. Use your active cognition and problem-solving skills.
- Fall back on your planned response. You should have this practiced into your procedural memory.
- Breathe. Send the message to your brain, body, and central nervous system that you are safe.
- Work to establish a relationship and connection.
- Listen. Repeat back what you hear.
- Think about the ways you can reduce the anxiety, anger, or presenting emotion.
- Find ways to help get their cognition online. (Example: I might say, "Wow, that's a cool shirt. What color is it?" because they are forced to pull out of panic and think about what color they are wearing. It forces that active cognition back online.)

- Speak in terms of being sincerely sorry about what has upset them. Validate that feeling of being wronged. Make sure they feel heard by you.
- Brainstorm a way to make the situation better. Offer a solution.
- Not every situation can be diffused. Know when to call law enforcement.

Holding Offenders Accountable

It is important to think through some of the key points on offender accountability, especially as it relates to our faith communities. Here are a few of the most crucial things we must consider:

- One of the most important things we can do is hold offenders accountable for their inappropriate violent actions.
- When we hold offenders accountable, this *is* the most loving thing we can do. It is the most loving thing for the offender and the victim.
- Actions have consequences. This is no different than what we teach toddlers.
- Accountability for being violent cuts abuser's ability to manipulate the situation and cause further harm to the victim (by using us).
- When we hold offenders accountable, we do not share information about the victim.
- When we hold offenders accountable, we are saying this is not acceptable in our community. We are saying people are valuable and do not deserve to be violated.
- Just because an abuser asks for forgiveness does not mean we can force a victim to accept their apology. That would not be holding an abuser or a victim accountable. That would be forcing a victim to be accountable for additional actions of the abuser. Just because forgiveness might be a positive action does not mean we can

force a victim to be accountable for the offender's positive action.

- When true change happens in an offender, there are distinct signs that go far beyond being sorry, repenting, and/
or crying. Examples include:
    - There is a change in how the person believes
    they are entitled to behave behind closed
    doors.
    - There is extensive time (years) without inap-
    propriate behavior.
    - The victim feels safe.
    - They take responsibility for the damage they
    caused (verbally, financially, and beyond).
    - They have learned tools and techniques on
    how to respond differently.
    - They practice responses that do not include
    hints of entitlement, power, or control.
- Offenders usually need specialized therapy and counseling that targets their motivations and views on women
and gender; helps them think through uses of power and
control; and challenges perceptions of entitlement.

Case Study: Arguing in the Car

James is getting ready for church when his wife, Brenda, drops
his breakfast on the floor.[14] He is livid. He was counting on that
food, and now she's ruined it. He walks back to his room, cursing
and screaming, while Brenda cleans the mess up off the floor.
James opens his closet door, shoves something in his pants, and
puts his suit jacket on. Brenda sees the bulge when he comes out
into the kitchen, ready to head to services.

---

14 The inspiration for this case study is from Chaplain James Bradley on
the AIMS Training and Consulting team.

They make their way toward the prominent church they attend, the one with more than two thousand members. James makes comments about her dress and hat and throws a tissue box at her. Finally, as they pull into the driveway of the church, Brenda loses it. She feels as if, this close to church, maybe she's safe enough to give James a piece of her mind. Surely he wouldn't do anything here at church. He wouldn't want the pastor to see him like that.

Brenda starts yelling at the top of her lungs at James, who looks mortified and traumatized. The ushers notice and start to whisper among themselves. They think Brenda must be quite a problem. James tightens his jaw, tells Brenda she's a worthless wife, and opens the car door. Brenda opens her car door and starts walking, without James, to the church. They are parked about four rows back.

Before anyone knows what is happening, James leans against the car, draws a weapon out of his jacket, and starts firing. Brenda goes down almost immediately, and the ushers start running around in a panic.

1. What do you do first?
2. What is your address when you call for emergency services?
3. Do the ushers have a plan for this? What is it?
4. What do you do with James? How do you keep him from shooting anyone else?
5. What can you do for Brenda?
6. How do you react to the rest of the congregation already in the building? What about the parking lot?
7. How do you protect the pastor and the pastor's family and other staff and their families?
8. Is the nursery and kids' area secure?

Acknowledgments

A book on a difficult topic such as this would not be possible without hundreds of folks standing with me. I am forever grateful to the people who invested time and energy into helping to make this book happen, and I would like to thank the following individuals:

Dr. Karen Strand Winslow, who connected me with the publisher, insisting this needed to be in print for everyone to access. Dr. Kathy Armistead and Jennifer Manley Rogers, who worked tirelessly on this project, and Shelly Beach, who believed in this book (and in me as a writer) before I had the courage and brain power to start it, as well as Dr. Jeanne Hoeft, for guiding the early process in doctorate studies.

My training team for Church Safety Seminars at American Institute for Management Strategies (AIMS), including Chief Anthony Williams, Repaula Tate, Dr. William "Edward" Smith, Marieta (Mo) Oglesby, and Chaplain James Bradley. Chapter 6 could not have happened without their wisdom.

My local Starbucks friends, who provided my writing seat and endless supply of coffee and tea (I love you, Inwood and Willow). The survivors who I cannot list but who inspire me daily as well as those who were my own service providers when I was in a shelter and healing.

My family, who put up with me writing an entire dissertation and then a book; especially my little girl, whose first written sentence was "Mom is editing," and my son, who is becoming a young man who values and respects women and whose strength and resilience give me courage.

Kim Feeney, who spent extensive time reviewing and helping with chapter 5 to make sure grant information was correct and easy to understand. Dr. Josh Arduengo, for his work in reviewing the neurobiology portions.

My core team of pastors who have me on speed dial to consult with them about issues of domestic violence and sexual assault; I could not have done this without their voices and contribution, especially Dan Masshardt, Mike Schutz, Aimee Stone Cooper, Amy Cooper Heckman, Daniel Lemke, Jeff Brady, Mike Yost, Taryn Eudaly, Brandy Betts, and Janel Apps Ramsey.

The Collin County Council on Family Violence through the Junior League of Collin County, especially Tonia Cunningham, Haleh Cochran, Hind Jarrah, Mirjana Senad Omeragic, Joanie Stephens, and Patricia Hinojos. The team of prosecutors in the Domestic Violence Unit at the Collin County District Attorney's Office, under Greg Willis's leadership, who have all been anxiously awaiting this book. My local service providers, The Turning Point Rape Crisis Center (Wendy Hannah), as well as Hope Rising (Lisa Miller and folks), and the one I call "my victim advocate," because I always call on her to help me with survivor care, Gaye Gardner.

The Kansas Coalition Against Sexual and Domestic Violence (KCSDV) where I served as the Accreditation and Technical Assistance Coordinator and learned so much. Especially Joyce Grover, Kathy Ray, Sara Rust-Martin, Janene Radke, Rachel Gardner, and Laura Patzner.

My fellow advocates and workers in this field, including Leslie Morgan Steiner, Pamela Jacobs, Becky Davis, Misty Campbell, Jeri

Nicole, Mary Stolz, Megan McFarrell, Kristina Scott, Shelly Sanders Newman, Melissa Miller DeDonder, Michelle McCormick, Monica Phinney, Tanya Day, Whitney Lozenski, Justin Shaw, Michael Munson, Julie Owens, David Hayward, Kelsey McKay, Russell Strand, Mark Wynn, David Lisak, Jackson Katz, Ally Kern, Cheryl Bowles Summers, Ashley Easter, Ryan Ashton, Mandy Marshall, Natalie Collins, Kim Day, Olga Trujillo, and so many more. The A Window Between Worlds staff, especially my "other" Christy, Christy Turek.

And, finally, I want to remember my friend and fellow advocate at the Wichita Area Sexual Assault Center, Pearla Rodriguez, who was taken from us by the very thing we give our lives to prevent every single day. We think of you often and miss you dearly.

Appendices

Appendix A: Top 10 Things Pastors Are Most Shocked to Learn

1. **Many incidents of abuse are not illegal.**
   To hold power and control over someone means that the smallest, seemingly insignificant things can be used. For example, when an abuser clenches their fists when angry, this could send the message to the victim that the abuse is capable of using those fists to cause harm. Or when the perpetrator uses their body to physically intimidate the victim, it sends the message the perpetrator is in control. However, none of these things are going to get someone jail time. It is not nice to tower over someone or clench your fists around them, but it is not illegal.

2. **Physical abuse is much more than being punched, shot, kicked, or stabbed.**
   Physical abuse is anything that involves the body. This can include body-to-body contact, weapons, or neither. It could mean using the body to tower over someone or block them in the room. Physical abuse could mean forcing someone to stay awake at night and listen to them.

Or it could be throwing things at another person, jumping out of a moving car when angry, driving recklessly, or anything that might cause harm to the physical body.

3. **Couples counseling is *not* a good idea when power and control is an issue.**

   Couples counseling involves both parties having a voice and sharing how both feel about various things. This is a terrible idea for many reasons. Among these are the fact that one party will not be allowed to share honestly, and if that party does decide to share honestly, they could pay severely for it later. When power and control is an issue, each person involved needs individual counseling, and the perpetrator needs specialized counseling that focuses on offender accountability and learning to behave in more appropriate ways.

4. **The forensic exam is more about medical care than collecting evidence.**

   A SANE's (Sexual Assault Nurse Examiner's) primary role is patient care. Forensic collection is a part of what a SANE does but not the main task. A SANE is a nurse first, and thus cares for their patient's medical needs above all else.

5. **The consequences of violence (even death) are the result of the offender's actions and no one else's.**

   If a person dies at the hands of a perpetrator, it is the perpetrator's fault. It is not the victim's friends' fault. It is not the victim's family's fault. It is not your fault. This action happened at the hands of the offender. This is important because as faith leaders we model for survivors what it means to not accept responsibility for actions we cannot control.

6. **Protection orders require additional effort to obtain approval.**

   Prior to being issued, protection orders require that extensive paperwork be filled out, and there must be a strong case for a judge to accept it. Why is it so difficult? Because the initial protection order is *ex parte*, meaning it is without one party. In United States law, due process indicates that everyone has a right to fair treatment, including being able to share their side. When a protection order is issued *ex parte*, it is without the knowledge, consent, or opinion of one party. Thus, judges take this very seriously. If they violate the rights of one party, they need sufficient and adequate reason to do so. For an *ex parte* protection order to be issued there must be sufficient evidence that immediate harm is probable. However, if a person is not granted their initial *ex parte* request, they may still receive a court date for both parties to be present and argue their side, after which a protection order (that is not *ex parte*) may be issued.

7. **Forgiveness is one of the most painful topics for victims.**

    Forgiveness might be a faith leader's favorite topic, but it is a source of great pain and agony for a survivor of violence. Victims feel pressured to take responsibility for the horrific actions that were done to them, against their will, by again forgiving against their will. For more about survivor care regarding forgiveness, see the Q & A with Pastor Chantel in chapter 3.

8. **Most crimes of domestic violence and sexual assault are not reported or prosecuted.**

    Faith leaders often assume that when an assault happens the victim reports it, there is a trial, and the offender is locked away. Statistics indicate that nothing could be further from the truth. One of my colleagues is an adult women's domestic violence counselor, and she guessed that only about 10 percent of the women that sit in her chair have ever reported the violence that happened to them. I believe her, since David Lisak reports that anywhere from 64 to 96 percent of rapes are never reported.[1] The criminal justice system, prosecutors, law enforcement, and others are doing their best to hold offenders accountable and protect victims. The statistics suggest we have a long way to go.

9. **Protection orders, divorce decrees, and custody arrangements should be kept on file in the church office.**

   Family violence can be one of the worst issues to deal with on church grounds. If there is a custody arrangement, the children's department needs to know about it. If there is an active protection order, the police will need it if they are called to the scene. All of these important documents should be filed in the church office. However, remember issues of confidentiality and consent when you store documents and keep them in a safe location.

10. **Two people cannot abuse each other.**

    Abuse happens when one person exerts power over another in order to control the outcome of activities and events through the use of actions, words, or innuendoes. Thus, one person abuses another person. Two people do not control each other. There is no such thing as mutual abuse. If you see something that looks like mutual abuse, the chances are that one person is perpetrating the violence and one person is reacting to that violence (even if it is in a way that appears to be violent).

---

1   According to Fisher, Cullen, & Turner, 2000; National Crime Victim's Center, 1992; Perkins & Klaus, 1996; Russell, 1982, in David Lisak and Paul M. Miller, "Repeat Rape and Multiple Offending among Undetected Rapists," *Violence and Victims* 127, no. 1 (2002): 73, http://www.davidlisak.com/wp-content/uploads/pdf/RepeatRapein UndetectedRapists.pdf.

Appendix B: Top 10 Things You Can Do for Survivors

1. **Find ways to help the person to see their strength and value.**

   When a person admits they were abused, we can automatically assume they are strong. All we need to do is help them see the strength already there. For example, it takes an unbelievable strength to deal with other people's reactions, which, if we are honest, are often not very loving responses. It also takes incredible resilience to actually leave the abusive situation. Anyone who has the strength to give up their house and all possessions to live in a shelter, who has nothing but the clothes on their back, and who gives up their status in society, and sometimes their job, is incredibly strong.

   The truth is, the strength and power are already there. Survivors are incredibly strong. They just need to realize it, and we can help point it out to them.

2. **Begin your conversation to a victim with safe statements.** Use preferred statements such as, "I am so sorry; you do not deserve that," or "This must be really difficult"; but pair them with words that seek to really connect with the survivor, such as, "Tell me more about what is going on with you." Victims are intelligent and see through the times people treat them like a problem or throw out words simply because it is the right thing to say. It takes effort to connect with a survivor and really understand where they are. Find words and phrases that communicate that you want to connect and understand.

3. **When appropriate, find ways to make the invisible scars visible.**

   A lot of abuse is not visible. Often a survivor cannot point to the wound and say, "There it is, that is how I was abused." When you cannot point to a bruise and say,

"They did this to me," it is so easy to deny it ever happened. But when we help make invisible scars tangible, we can help them see it, identify it, and heal from it.

How do we actually turn the invisible visible?

- First, believe the story when it is shared.
- Second, listen to the story, sometimes more than once. The more a person tells their story, the more power they have over it.
- Third, let the person find themselves in the telling of the story.

4. **Give empathy, not sympathy.**

Brené Brown gives suggestions on offering genuine, heartfelt empathy. She says empathy is "the skill or ability to tap into our own experiences in order to connect with an experience someone is relating to us."[2] Empathy requires dealing with our own feelings of shame and pain to feel what another person feels. It means facing the times where you felt dehumanized. It means confronting the times when you may have been abused. It means actually feeling and sensing the pain of another person through your own previous experience. Empathy is challenging because you have to maintain your objectivity while feeling with people, but it is an essential component to connecting with trauma survivors.

5. **Use effective communication skills.**

This requires that a person listen, and really listen. It also means making effective use of appropriate body language. Lean forward to show you are actually interested in what is being shared. Keep eye contact. Nod when you understand. Ask clarifying questions when you do not understand. Engage fully in the conversation as an active listener.

---

2   Brené Brown, *I Thought It Was Just Me*, 33.

6. **Put aside judgments.**

If you have not personally been victimized, terrorized, or harmed by someone you love and trust, it is nearly impossible to know what it feels like. Even if someone you love has experienced this trauma, it does not mean you fully understand this experience. Without living through it yourself, it is difficult to form an idea of how you would behave if you were caught in cycles of abuse. You might be surprised at how you behave.

Judgments break trust. Judgments create a barrier between yourself and the victim's empowerment from you. Put aside judgments and just be present in the moment.

7. **Check your bias.**

Some common biases that I encounter about victims of domestic violence and sexual assault are things like:

- Most people lie about assault.
- Abusers are vicious monsters.
- Emotional abuse is not that bad.

None of these biases (and many others) are helpful when dealing with survivors. Try to put aside the things you automatically believe about victims and violence.

8. **Be a consistent, active presence.**

When you are a consistent presence in the person's life, it shows you are reliable and not going to disappear when things get tough. It is entirely possible that the survivor is only telling you a small part to test if you can handle it or if you will run away screaming. The victim might also push you away on purpose but stay consistent and patient. How can you be consistently present? Send a text or email every so often to see how they are doing. Call and check on them. Say hi on social media. Do what you can to be an active and consistent presence.

9. **Take care of yourself.**

   It is equally important to take care of yourself. Be present, be active, and listen to the abuse in consistent intervals, but make time for yourself as well.

10. **Remember your position of power.**

    Take time to recognize your own privilege. As the person hearing the story of violence and abuse, you have a certain amount of power in holding the narrative.

Appendix C: Top 10 Ways to Communicate Openness to Victims

How can we communicate to people involved in our ministries that they will not be neglected, rejected, or accused if they come to us? How do we help them understand that there are ways we can help them and that we want to offer assistance?

1. Post safety cards in the bathroom or on the back of stall doors with info on how to get help. This sends the message that this church takes abuse seriously.
2. Preach about domestic violence and sexual assault from the pulpit. Talk about how violence and abuse is unacceptable and no one deserves to be abused.
3. Talk to the congregation in terms of "there are worse things than divorce and breakups"; for example, being trapped in an abusive relationship.
4. Talk about sexual assault during April, which is Sexual Assault Awareness Month (SAAM).
5. Talk about domestic violence in October. It's Domestic Violence Awareness Month (DVAM).
6. When you tell stories in your sermons, find ways to work in how violence is never acceptable and no one deserves to be violated.
7. Talk about healthy bodies and healthy relationships in sermons. Include youth in age-appropriate ways.

8. Include bulletin inserts about how to find help for abuse and violence in your area.
9. Have resources and brochures available on service providers in your area.
10. Bring people from your local service providers in to speak to your congregation. If they are grant funded, they are probably required to have community education and presentations available.

Appendix D: Top 10 Things *Not* to Say to a Survivor of Violence

1. This must be God's will.
2. Time heals all wounds.
3. Forgive and forget.
4. God won't give you more than you can handle.
5. What did you do to upset them?
6. There are two sides to every story.
7. You need to take responsibility for your part in all this.
8. But they are such a great person. They can't be all bad. I'm sure they meant well.
9. Are you sure it's really abuse? Are there marks?
10. I tried to tell you. What did you expect?

Appendix E: Top 10 Things *to* Say to a Survivor of Violence

1. I am here. I'm present.
2. I care.
3. I believe you.
4. What do you need? How can I help? Can we watch your kids? How about a gas card?
5. I am so glad you told me.
6. You do not deserve that. No matter what.
7. I'll be here for you.
8. Thank you for trusting me.

9. What are you thinking and feeling?
10. It is not your fault.

Appendix F: Active Listening with Victims

If we are actively listening to another person, we are participating in the moment with them. There are several components of active listening to remember and consider.

1. Consider how you might stop your own internal conversation and listen to the words being said.
2. Be conscious of your own bias and preference.
3. Stop figuring out what you will say next and simply hear and observe the present.
4. Watch for verbal and nonverbal cues.
5. Be comfortable with silence.
6. Promote a safe environment.
7. Accept the other person's voice as it is.
8. Validate the strengths you witness.
9. Acknowledge the feelings you hear.
10. Bear witness to the story by feeling with the person.

Steps for Active Listening

Connect

- Allow yourself to feel with them.
- Figure out how to connect human to human.
- Make eye contact.
- Look at them while they speak.
- Use nods and smiles to show you are engaged.
- Put away the phone.
- Validate their words with your body language.

Understand

- Say, "What I hear you saying is . . ."
- Listen for what is not said.

- What within their words can you demonstrate and reflect back that you are understanding what they are saying?
- What does their body language say?
- Set aside preconceived notions.
- Identify what emotions are present and affirm them.
- Examples: "It sounds like that is really exhausting" or "I can imagine that would be overwhelming."

Be Present

- Be in the moment.
- Don't think about what you will say when they stop speaking; just be present, fully listening to the person.
- Listen more than you talk.

Reframe

- When appropriate, reframe to highlight their strength. Example: "I'm such an idiot. I should have left earlier" can become "I see the strength it took you to take care of your child through all of this."

Do Not Problem-solve

- Now is not the time to start analyzing the problem and figure out solutions. It is time to listen and engage. If any problem solving is done during this time, it is about safety—and safety only.

Appendix G: Safety Planning Basics

Although safety planning should be done with a professional who understands the dynamics of domestic violence and sexual assault, there are times when you will be the only person available to help a survivor think through safety planning. Here are some tips:

1. Help the person finish these sentences:

   - If I need to leave quickly, I will . . .

- The safest place in my house is . . .
- The person closest to me I can tell about my fears
  is . . .

2. Do the children's teachers know?
3. Do the children know how to call for help? Can they develop a code word with the children so they know to get out?
4. Do colleagues at work know there is a concern? Are they safe in the parking lot?
5. What is the twenty-four-hour hotline in your area?
6. Can the locks be changed? Steel doors put in?
7. Where is the protection order? Can a copy be kept in the glove box?
8. Stash away the following (with a friend or family member—or in the trunk of the car):

- phone charger
- money
- feminine products
- Social Security cards
- court documents
- insurance
- credit cards
- birth certificates
- medication
- jewelry
- immunization papers
- extra clothes
- immigration papers
- passport/license
- kids' favorite toys/
  stuffed animals

9. Know where keys are at all times.
10. Encourage the person at risk to trust their gut—even if it does not seem to make sense. The body tends to know when danger is imminent.

Appendix H: Crisis Moment Checklist

If you are on the scene where a person is traumatized and you don't know what to do, remember:

- Chances are they will not remember what you say or do but will remember that you were present (and it is possible they will not remember that).
- Do not try to help figure out the next steps. Not yet. They cannot cognitively go there in crisis moments.
- Be aware of your body position. Don't tower over the person. Put your body in a more vulnerable position.
- Do not touch victims without asking.
- You hold the power, just by the nature of your position.
- Listen to your gut and trust it.
- Practice active listening.

Appendix I: False Reporting Statistics

False reporting of assault is about as common as false allegations of theft and of every other crime. In other words, it does not happen often. But when it does, it tends to be so devastating and life-altering for the accused that we jump to protect those who might be false suspects. Unfortunately, the statistics suggest that we jump to protect the offender instead of the victim.

The best resources we have indicate that only from 2 to 10 percent of those who report assault are making it up (or it is a false report). This means, at the very worst, that there is a 90 percent chance the person disclosing assault to you is telling the truth.

Below is a list of the best resources and research on false reporting statistics. For an overview of false reporting from the National Sexual Violence Resource Center, research and compilation funded by the Office of Violence Against Women, see www.nsvrc.org/sites/default/files/Publications_NSVRC_Overview_False-Reporting.pdf. The highlights of this overview report include:

a. "The majority of sexual assaults, an estimated 63 percent, are never reported to the police (Rennison, 2002)."

b. A false report is defined as: "a reported crime to a law enforcement agency that an investigation factually proves never occurred."

c. In 2006 a team of researchers studied 812 reports of assault for the period 2000–2003 and "found a 2.1 percent rate of false reports (Heenan & Murray 2006)."

d. In 2010 Dr. David Lisak and his team of researchers studied 136 assault cases in Boston from the years 1998–2007 and "found a 5.9 percent rate of false reports (Lisak et al., 2010)."

e. "Misconceptions about false reporting rates have direct, negative consequences and can contribute to why many victims don't report sexual assaults (Lisak et al., 2010)."

Dr. David Lisak and researchers authored an important paper on false reporting that was published in 2010 in the journal *Violence Against Women*.[3] It is currently available to read at www .icdv.idaho.gov/conference/handouts/False-Allegations.pdf. Highlights from this paper include:

a. "For centuries, it has been asserted and assumed that women 'cry rape,' that a large proportion of rape allegations are maliciously concocted for purposes of revenge or other motives."

b. "The heated public discourse about the frequency of false rape allegations often makes no reference to actual research."

c. For a reported sexual assault to be considered "false," there must be evidence the assault never happened.

d. In this study, "Of the 136 cases of sexual assault 8 (5.9%) were coded as false reports, 61 (44.9%) did not proceed

---

3   David Lisak, Lori Gardinier, Sarah C. Nicksa, and Ashley M. Cote, "False Allegations of Sexual Assault: An Analysis of Ten Years of Reported Cases," *Violence Against Women* 16, no. 12 (2010): 1318–34, www .icdv.idaho.gov/conference/handouts/False-Allegations.pdf.

to any prosecution or disciplinary action, 48 (35.3%) were referred for prosecution or disciplinary action, and 19 (13.9%) contained insufficient information to be coded."

David Lisak created his own fact sheet on false reporting. This is available at www.thurstondvsataskforce.com/docs/materials /false-allegations-of-rape-fact-sheet.pdf. Highlights include discussing six credible studies from the period 1977–2009. In those studies, the following statistics were discovered about false reports:

a. The first study recorded 6 percent false allegations.
b. In the second study 8.3 percent were false.
c. The third study was done in England and Wales and discovered 10.9 percent were false.
d. The fourth is the "largest and most comprehensive study," and only 2.5 percent were considered false allegations.
e. The fifth report was done in Australia, and 2.1 percent were false reports.
f. The final report Lisak shares (which was his study completed in 2009) indicates 5.9 percent false reports.
g. For a compilation of best resources from End Violence Against Women International (EVAWI), see www .evawintl.org/Best-Practices/FAQs.

The most important thing to glean from these studies and statistics is that the chances are very high that a person disclosing an experience of assault is telling you the truth. It is a far greater risk to believe the person before you is among the potential 10 percent who lie than to jeopardize belief with the 90 percent.

Appendix J: Domestic Violence Decision Tree—A Starting Point When You Don't Know What to Do

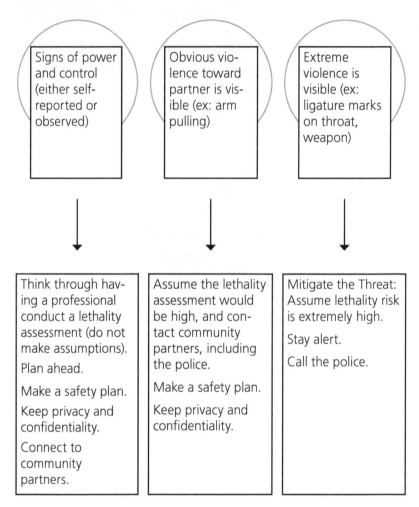

Preventing Extreme Violence

Have escorts from the parking lot. Do background checks. Have ushers/greeters and a safety team trained. Keep court documents on file. Develop a policy on how to handle these issues. Keep the building well lit. Know your entry and exit points.

Appendix K: Questions to Consider When Making Decisions about Domestic Violence and Sexual Assault

1. Do you know the facts? What are the facts? Can you write them out and see what is a fact and what is not?
2. What are the things you suspect but do not know for sure? Know the difference between what you know to be true and assumptions being made.
3. Is money, power, or position affecting how you feel or think? If it is, why do you think that is?
4. Do you have any biases that need to be confronted? Are you assuming anything about persons involved?
5. What are the positives in this situation? What are the negatives? Do you have any control to assist in highlighting the positives?
6. Does someone feel threatened? Who is it, and what is the threat? If it is a life threating situation, call your community partners immediately.
7. Can you formulate an action plan (step one, step two, step three)? For example, when this happens, I will do this first. I will say this second (and so forth). Thinking about it ahead of time will help when you are in the intensity of trauma.
8. Who can you call for advice, guidance, and support? Remember confidentiality, but who can support you?
9. Who does not feel safe? What do you need to do about this?
10. Will what you plan to do make things better? How do you know it will help?

Appendix L: National Hotlines

The United States national twenty-four-hour hotlines are always available.

- Phone: 1-800-799-7233
- Phone TTY: 1-800-787-3224
- Phone in Spanish: 1-800-799-7233
- 24-hr. bilingual domestic violence helpline: 651-772-1611 (from Casa Esperanza)
- Website (with an online chat available): www.thehotline .org/.
- For Youth: www.loveisrespect.org/. Text: loveis to 22522.

Appendix M: Websites

Domestic Violence

Family Violence and Custody: www.ncjfcj.org/our-work/domestic -violence.

Health and Domestic Violence (through Futures Without Violence): www.futureswithoutviolence.org/health/national-health -resource-center-on-domestic-violence/.

Health and Intimate Partner Violence: http://ipvhealth.org/.

National Domestic Violence Hotline: www.thehotline.org.

National Network to End Domestic Violence: https://nnedv.org/.

National Resource Center on Domestic Violence: www.nrcdv.org/.

State Coalitions: https://nnedv.org/content/state-u-s-territory -coalitions/.

Sexual Assault

Campus Sexual Assault: www.acha.org/ACHA/Resources/Topics /Violence.aspx.

National Sexual Violence Resource Center: www.nsvrc.org/.

RAINN (Rape, Abuse, Incest National Network): www.rainn.org.

Legal

AEquitas (prosecutors' resource): www.aequitasresource.org/.

Danger/Risk Assessment: www.womenslaw.org/danger-assessment.

Legal Information by State: www.womenslaw.org/laws.

Legal Momentum's National Judicial Education Program: www
.njep-ipsacourse.org/.

Women's Law: www.womenslaw.org/.

Miscellaneous

American Academy of Orthopedic Surgeons List of Family Violence State Laws: www.aaos.org/CustomTemplates/Content
.aspx?id=22253&ssopc=1.

Battered Women's Justice Project: www.bwjp.org/.

End Violence Against Women International (EVAWI): www.evaw
intl.org/.

Financial Management Curriculum: https://nnedv.org/content
/economic-justice-curriculum/.

Futures Without Violence: www.futureswithoutviolence.org/.

Gender-Based Violence (a project of the National Resource Center on Domestic Violence): https://vawnet.org/.

Immigration, National Immigrant Women's Advocacy Project:
www.niwap.org/.

Latin@s Network (National): https://casadeesperanza.org/.

LGBT National Hotline: www.glbtnationalhelpcenter.org/.

Male Survivors, 1 in 6: https://1in6.org/.

Male Survivors Support: www.malesurvivor.org/index.php.

No More: https://nomore.org/.

Resource Sharing Project: www.resourcesharingproject.org/.

Stalking Awareness Month: http://stalkingawarenessmonth.org
/about.

Stalking Resource Center: http://victimsofcrime.org/our-programs
/stalking-resource-center (Note: This will soon be under
AEquitas and the weblink may change).

Tech Safety: www.techsafety.org/.

Technology Safety Toolkit: www.techsafety.org/confidentiality.

Teen Dating Violence: www.loveisrespect.org. Texting Available:
Text "loveis" to 22522.

Title IX Information (through End Rape on Campus): http://end rapeoncampus.org/title-ix/.

Transgender Resource, Forge Forward: National Resource: http://forge-forward.org/.

Trauma and Mental Health (The National Center on Domestic Violence, Trauma and Mental Health): www.nationalcenterdv traumamh.org/.

Women of Color Network: www.wocninc.org/.

United States Government

Campus Sexual Assault: www.justice.gov/ovw/protecting-students -sexual-assault.

Campus Sexual Assault, Dear Colleague Letter: www2.ed.gov/about /offices/list/ocr/letters/colleague-201104.html.

Center for Disease Control (CDC): www.cdc.gov/violenceprevention /index.html.

Office of Victims of Crime: https://ovc.ncjrs.gov/topic.aspx?topic id=27.

Office of Violence Against Women: www.justice.gov/ovw/domestic -violence.

Stalking: www.justice.gov/ovw/stalking.

Title IX: www2.ed.gov/about/offices/list/ocr/docs/tix_dis.html.

The U.S. Department of Justice: www.justice.gov/.

CPSIA information can be obtained
at www.ICGtesting.com
Printed in the USA
LVHW011201071218
599543LV00004B/29/P